THE BEST
IS NOT
TOO GOOD
FOR YOU

New Approaches to Public Collections in England

contemporary
art society

Whitechapel Gallery

THE BEST
IS NOT
TOO GOOD
FOR YOU

Contents

Foreword

In 2013 two municipal authorities on either side of the Atlantic triggered outrage as they announced the sell-off of publicly-owned works of art. Officials in Croydon, a suburb of London, decided to auction 24 valuable bowls and vases from a collection of Chinese ceramics dating from 2,500 BC to the eighteenth century. In Detroit, a bankrupted local government hired Christie's to appraise the African, American, European and Oceanic masterpieces held by the Detroit Institute of Art (DIA). Fierce public campaigning and a surge of public giving rescued the collections of the DIA; the people of Croydon were not so lucky. Their ceramics were duly sold off, in fact failing to realise the millions envisaged by local officials. At the time of writing, the London Borough of Tower Hamlets is set to follow suit by selling a monumental Henry Moore sculpture.

An unexpected consequence of these events is the sudden realisation that we have been living with great treasures that we have not just taken for granted, but failed to notice. Such is often the fate of the local museum collection. This book reveals that there are remarkable treasures to be found in our regional museums, art and artefacts that can contribute entirely new readings to canonical art histories. They represent communities, they depict landscapes and cities, they are also symptomatic of the ideological and aesthetic preoccupations of an age.

The history and politics of collecting in Britain are complex. Although aristocratic patronage had led to the establishment of important collections of Antiquities and Old Masters, these holdings remained private until the nineteenth century with the founding of the National Gallery. It was with the rise of industrialisation that private individuals came to establish local institutions and to bequeath their holdings to the public. Unlike North America where individuals would typically endow institutions, civic museums in twentieth century Britain have been,

in the main, supported by a combination of centralised, state and local government support.

Their fortunes have risen and fallen in line with public finance. Yet these often beleaguered local museums have, over the years, built up breathtaking collections with a distinctive regional character. Charities and individuals have made crucial contributions to financing acquisitions, but they have tended towards works endorsed by history. The organisation that has enabled regional curators to take the great gamble of acquiring the art of our time has been the Contemporary Art Society.

This publication brings together the work of the Whitechapel Gallery and the Contemporary Art Society, two organisations whose collective mission is to enhance the public's engagement with art. Over twelve months, working across four displays, the Whitechapel Gallery and the Contemporary Art Society developed a unique collaboration, which showcases a selection of historic, modern and contemporary works of art from regional museums held in four different regions of England: the North West, East Coast, Midlands and the South.

The project grew out of the in-depth research of four invited curatorial fellows, each of whom was hosted by a different regional museum. These were, respectively, Anna Colin at the Harris Museum & Art Gallery, Preston; Helen Kaplinsky at the Ferens Art Gallery, Hull; Ingrid Swenson at the Wolverhampton Art Gallery and Gaia Tedone at the Royal Pavilion & Museums, Brighton & Hove.

The collaboration began with an invitation from the Whitechapel Gallery, which in recent years has developed an annual programme that provides a platform for public or private collections to be seen, enjoyed and debated with new audiences. The Contemporary Art Society has developed public collections of contemporary art across the UK for more than 100 years, donating over 8,000 works by contemporary artists to museums and public galleries, to be enjoyed in perpetuity. The two institutions were both founded in the first decade of the twentieth century; at a time when the art world was so small compared to the present, it is unsurprising that the same figures featured large in both histories. Charles Aitken was the first Director of the Whitechapel Gallery from 1901, and went on to be first Keeper, and then Director of the Tate Gallery from 1917. Aitken, together with the critic Roger Fry and the painter, writer and critic D.S. MacColl, who was Keeper of the Tate Gallery from 1906 to 1911, was the co-founder of the Contemporary Art Society in 1910. The writer and curator Bryan Robertson, who was Director of the Whitechapel Gallery from 1952 to 1968, was also a distinguished and energetic member of the committee of the Contemporary Art Society.

Although the Contemporary Art Society's purpose has always been the purchasing of contemporary art, it has also in the past made some noteworthy exhibitions. Between 1953 and 1958 three very successful exhibitions were initiated at the Tate Gallery and then toured the UK, introducing the work of upcoming artists to audiences outside London. In 1963 the Contemporary Art Society mounted an exhibition, shown simultaneously at the Whitechapel and Tate Galleries. 'British Painting in the Sixties' included work by the young and newly famous David Hockney, with a second exhibition 'British Sculpture in the Sixties' following in 1965.

The impetus for the research behind each of the current displays at the Whitechapel Gallery was the notion of philanthropy. The Contemporary Art Society pioneered the philanthropic support of contemporary artists for public collections at the beginning of the last century. Although state funding has increased in the interim, private funding of the arts is a central part of government discourse in 2014, and more broadly a subject of much critical debate. We believed this would be a rich starting point from which to explore the economy of the arts today.

Each fellow was subsequently tasked with a different focus within this overarching theme. For Anna Colin in the North West, the emphasis was to consider how local economics had influenced the holdings of regional collections. On the East Coast, Helen Kaplinsky was asked to consider how local art schools had shaped holdings in the region, while the fellow for the Midlands, Ingrid Swenson, considered the notion of perceived and actual value, focusing on ceramics and Pop Art. The fourth fellow,

Gaia Tedone, looked at the role of individuals in influencing the formation of collections in the South of England. Ultimately, it is the individual, whether an artist, curator, philanthropist or collector, whose passion and knowledge informs, shapes, develops and interprets collections.

Each of the four fellows has contributed an essay that explores areas of research and unfolds the ideas behind each display. We also invited two key figures to help open up the context of collecting to a broader audience. Specifically, Helen Rees Leahy, Senior Lecturer and Director of The Centre for Museology at The University of Manchester, provides an historical perspective on the relationship between philanthropy and the development of museum collections, while artist Matthew Darbyshire looks at collecting as a form of artistic practice.

We would like to thank the four curatorial fellows Anna Colin, Helen Kaplinsky, Ingrid Swenson and Gaia Tedone for their inspired selections. We are grateful to the lenders and their tireless staff working across the country, who are listed in full in the back pages. We are indebted to Arts Council England and the Paul Mellon Centre for Studies in British Art for enabling this collaboration, and to Kirsty Ogg and Lucy Bayley for moulding the project from its genesis, Candy Stobbs for pushing ahead on delivery and to Omar Kholeif and Christine Takengny for working to oversee its completion.

Unlike the Kunsthalle, the collecting museum accumulates a narrative over time. Displays drawn from these collections can ride across historical periods, swooping through ages and sensibilities to reveal unexpected commonalities. For visitors to the Whitechapel Gallery it is the encyclopaedic scope of the museum collection that is so appealing. Regardless of whether you seek out the shock of the new or return to admire the already known, there is something for everyone. This breadth also guarantees an encounter with the unexpected. This is what makes the encounter with a collection display such a great adventure. Let's hope that these programmes persuade our elected representatives that local collections are the lifeblood of our cultural patrimony.

Iwona Blazwick, Director, Whitechapel Gallery
Caroline Douglas, Director, Contemporary Art Society

The Art of Giving and Receiving
Helen Rees Leahy

The politics of austerity in contemporary Britain have without doubt re-activated a long-running debate about the relationship between philanthropy and the arts. Questions such as 'how best to incentivise private giving?', and 'how to direct individual generosity towards the support of publicly funded organisations?' (as opposed to personal initiatives and pet projects) are as pressing today as they were a century ago. One difference is the number and diversity of subsidised cultural organisations today, including museums and galleries, which are feeling the very sharp pinch of diminishing grants and are being encouraged to consider philanthropy as a (partial, at least) solution to their financial shortfall. Whether or not a new generation of cultural philanthropists emerges in twenty-first century Britain as a result, a brief survey of past entanglements between donors and institutions offers some cautionary tales, as well as sources of inspiration, for the present.

From the birth of the museum age in Britain, government reluctance to intervene in the sphere of cultural provision produced a dependence on private citizens to open their purses and/or donate their collections. In 1753, Hans Sloane (physician and collector) bequeathed his renowned collection of natural history specimens and cultural artefacts to the nation on condition that, in return, his heirs would receive £20,000 (far less than the estimated value of the collection) from the state. Unwilling to make such a sum available from treasury funds, the government launched a national lottery and thus, from a combination of private generosity and the public appetite for gambling, the British Museum was established.

A similar preference for private initiative over state intervention was evident some seventy years later when persistent calls for the creation of a National Gallery finally became irresistible.[1] It was not only a question of government parsimony: the argument was that artistic taste was an essentially private matter, and that the state should only offer its support for the creation of public collections if there was evidence of demand from an art-loving public. In 1824, the collector George Beaumont promised to bequeath 16 paintings to the nation on condition that the government, in turn, bought the collection of John Julius Angerstein to form the basis of the national collection. Beaumont's offer was sufficient to persuade the treasury to purchase 38 of Angerstein's pictures for £57,000; it was a gesture that was intended as a spur to future philanthropists, rather than as a signal for further government funding. In his 1824 Budget speech, the then Chancellor of the Exchequer, Frederick Robinson, commented 'I am sanguine in my hope that the noble example [of Beaumont] would be followed by many similar acts... the result of which will be the establishment of a splendid Gallery, worthy of the nation.'[2]

1 Brandon Taylor, *Art for the Nation: Exhibitions and the London Public, 1747–2001*, Manchester University Press, Manchester, 1999.
2 Quoted in Gregory Martin, 'The Founding of the National Gallery in London' (9 parts: April – December), *Connoisseur*, Vols. CLXXXV–CLXXXVII, 1974. Pt. 2, p.27.

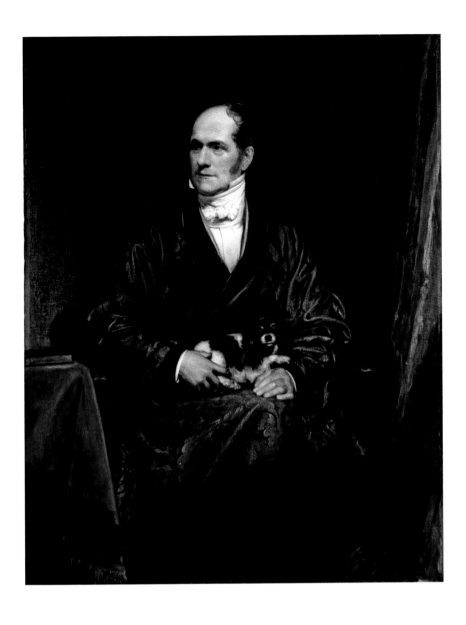

Arguably, the National Gallery's heavy dependence on donations in the ensuing years resulted in the unpredictable growth of the collection, so that by the 1850s the institution appeared amateurish, and its curatorial practices outdated compared with its counterparts in continental Europe.[3] In the absence of a coherent collecting strategy, the difficulty of saying 'no' to offers of artworks was already clear. As the National Gallery discovered, the problem was (and is) compounded when donations of art and/or money came with unwelcome strings attached. Inevitably, some philanthropists have their own ideas regarding the design, purpose and operation of public art galleries, while art purchases inevitably raise the vexed question of taste. A large fortune and a generous spirit are no guarantees that a donor's artistic inclinations will conform to the collecting preferences of public museums.

Robert Vernon, a successful horse and carriage supplier to the gentry and aristocracy, started to collect recent British art in the 1820s. Twenty years later, in 1847, he attempted

3 Parliamentary Select Committee on the National Gallery, 1853.

THE PROPOSED NATIONAL GALLERY OF BRITISH ART IN DANGER.

Mr. Henry Tate. "No, thank you, Mr. Red Tape, I don't want my Gifts to the Nation to be tied up by *you*, then packed away, and never seen again !"

to realise his ambition of founding a gallery of British Art by presenting 166 works to the National Gallery.[4] As the donation clearly fell outside the Gallery's collecting remit, and there was no desire on the part of the trustees to embrace recent British painting within its canon of historical art, Vernon's pictures were either displayed off-site or kept in store for the next 50 years: a continuing reminder of the divergent priorities of the giver and receiver.

The experience of the Vernon gift surely influenced the initially negative response to Henry Tate's offer to donate his collection (also of contemporary British art) to the National Gallery in 1889. Tate's offer came with the condition that the artworks should be displayed together as 'The Tate Collection'; this time, the trustees declined to accept. However, Tate was not a man to abandon the goal of placing his collection in the public realm. Eventually, after years of protracted negotiations with successive governments, Tate himself financed the building of a National Gallery of British Art (which quickly became known as the Tate Gallery) under the auspices of the National Gallery.[5] When the new gallery opened in 1897, both Tate and Vernon's collections were finally put on public exhibition, as each donor had desired.

4 Robin Hamlyn, *Robert Vernon's Gift: British Art for the Nation 1847,* Tate Publishing, London, 1993.
5 Taylor, op. cit.

The Art of Giving and Receiving

'The Proposed
National
Gallery of
British Art
in Danger',
Punch, 5
July 1890.
Reproduced
with permission
of Punch
Limited, www.
punch.co.uk

In the event, the creation of the Tate Gallery exacerbated tensions between artists, critics and gallery administrators over the selection of contemporary art that now formed part of the national collection. Opinion was particularly divided over the legacy of another arts philanthropist, the sculptor Francis Chantrey, who had died in 1841. Chantrey had bequeathed a substantial portion of his estate to the Royal Academy in order to create a fund for 'the purchase of works of fine art of the highest merit'. The selection of works bought with the proceeds of the Chantrey Bequest was administered by the Royal Academy, despite the fact that purchases now automatically entered the collection of the Tate Gallery. As the Chantrey Bequest was the primary conduit for acquisitions by the Tate, the refusal of the academicians to relinquish control of this vital source of patronage was galling to those who advocated a more expansive and less conservative approach to collecting.[6] One of the fiercest critics of the administration of the Chantrey Bequest was D.S. MacColl, who later became Keeper of the Tate Gallery (1906–11) and was one of the founders of the Contemporary Art Society in 1910.

The management of the Chantrey Bequest was just one of many pressures on public art collections in the first decade of the twentieth century. Disputes over competing approaches to art history, the skills required of museum curators, and the relationship between boards of trustees and their professional employees were as intense in 1910 as they are today.[7] In terms of acquisitions, there was insufficient money to compete in the transatlantic market for Old Masters, combined with a lack of institutional expertise and confidence to invest successfully in 'modern foreign' art, including the Impressionists and their successors. For many museum reformers, including the founders of the Contemporary Art Society, concerted action was needed both as a support and a rebuke to museums that were under-funded, but also lacking ambition. Unlike individuals such as Vernon and Tate, who had relied on personal wealth and generosity to shift institutional practice, both the Contemporary Art Society and the slightly older National Art Collections Fund (NACF) re-activated a nineteenth century model of associational campaigning and philanthropy. From the outset, the Contemporary Art Society adopted a developmental approach to acquisitions: works by young or advanced artists were bought, loaned for exhibitions in order to increase familiarity with them, and then distributed to public collections when a museum and its public were judged ready to appreciate them.

This cautious mechanism contrasted with the interventionist tactics occasionally employed by the NACF, which launched seven years earlier, in 1903. The early philanthropy of the NACF was a thinly veiled criticism of the perceived incompetence of the trustees of the National Gallery and their failure to attract adequate financial and political support to compete against private dealers and their overseas clients. The response of the NACF committee was to call for public subscriptions to fund acquisitions, as a counter to institutional inaction. In 1905, an editorial in *The Burlington Magazine* commented approvingly that, 'men of intelligence are taking the law into their own hands and doing what the State is always too busy to do.'[8] Later that year, the NACF launched its first major public appeal to purchase Velazquez's *Rokeby Venus* for the National Gallery.

The idea of raising funds by public subscription in order to supplement the purchase grants of the National Gallery had been mooted as early as 1900 by D.S. MacColl in an article entitled 'Friends of the National Gallery'. The idea was modelled on the Amis du Louvre, which, according to MacColl, was responsible for a number of valuable additions

6 Gordon Fyfe, *Art, Power and Modernity. English Art Institutions, 1750–1950*, Leicester University Press, Leicester, 2001.
7 Helen Rees Leahy, '"Scholarly and Disinterested": *The Burlington Magazine* 1903–1914', in Elizabeth Mansfield, *Art History and its Institutions*, Routledge, London, 2002, pp. 231–45.
8 Charles Holmes, 'Private Enterprise in Public Affairs', *The Burlington Magazine*, Vol. VII, 1905, p. 94.

to the French national collection: 'Each member pays an annual subscription, and it is the duty of the committee to mark down and stalk examples of painters who are badly wanted in the Louvre and quietly bag them when they come into the market...'[9]

The impetus and expertise of groups such as the NACF and Contemporary Art Society was grounded in connoisseurship and a commitment to the idea of art for art's sake. In short, they sought to lead taste, and their concerns were primarily aesthetic, rather than social. In this respect, their initiatives departed markedly from those of late-Victorian social reformers such as Thomas Horsfall in Manchester, and Samuel Barnett in Whitechapel, London. For Horsfall and Barnett, access to art was primarily a means to an end, rather than an end in itself.

In 1910, when the Contemporary Art Society was founded, Horsfall wrote: 'Art is not only a useful thing... but is, certainly for all dwellers in large towns, a necessary for health.'[10] From today's perspective, his prescription of a regular dose of art for the well-being of the inhabitants of Manchester sounds remarkably prescient. Horsfall's conviction of the social, developmental and moral value of cultural participation was based on the 'evidence' of his own remarkable art experiment: namely, the creation of Manchester Art Museum. Horsfall's museum opened in Ancoats, one of the poorest areas of the city, in 1886, and contained rooms dedicated to painting, sculpture, architecture, domestic arts and nature. The educational purpose of the enterprise was manifest in the detailed notes, labels, pamphlets and guided tours that explained the artworks to visitors, especially children. For both Horsfall and his mentor John Ruskin,

9 D.S. MacColl, 'Friends of the National Gallery', *The Saturday Review*, 1900, pp. 751–52.
10 Thomas Coglan Horsfall, *The Need for Art in Manchester*, 1910.

ART IN WHITECHAPEL—LOAN EXHIBITION OF PICTURES IN ST. JUDE'S SCHOOL HOUSE, COMMERCIAL STREET, E.

C.J. Staniland,
*Art in
Whitechapel,
Loan Exhibition
of Pictures
in St. Jude's
School House,
Commercial
Street, East.*
Illustration for
The Graphic,
22 November
1884, engraving
© Look
and Learn

it was self-evident that paintings could inspire religious faith and understanding through the depiction of the beauty of nature, as well as biblical scenes.[11]

It was a conviction shared by the Rev. Samuel Barnett and his wife Henrietta, who established the Whitechapel Fine Art Exhibitions in 1881. Barnett was rector of St. Jude's, Whitechapel, and his programme of annual art exhibitions ran until 1898, when work began on the creation of a permanent art gallery in Whitechapel. The success of the Barnetts' exhibitions, which were free and open daily until 10pm, mirrored the popularity of Horsfall's Art Museum in Manchester. And like Horsfall, they shared Ruskin's conviction that the highest purpose of art was spiritual, rather than merely aesthetic.[12] Easily dismissed as paternalistic by the art cognoscenti, then and now, Barnett and Horsfall nevertheless demonstrated the possibility of attracting a broad public for art exhibitions that were both accessible and informative.

History shows that the relationship between private philanthropy and public provision is complex; inevitably, the objectives of official bodies and art-loving individuals have not always converged in the past, and will not do so in the future. At times, philanthropists have led, rather than followed, institutional practice, in terms of artistic taste as well as public engagement. The focus of philanthropy has not necessarily been (or is) narrow. In the 1920s, Samuel Courtauld created a fund of £50,000 to enable the Tate Gallery belatedly to form a collection of Impressionist and Post-Impressionist works, at the same time as he was building his own substantial collection and serving on the Committee of the Contemporary Art Society (1924–48).[13] Meanwhile, the enduring value of membership organisations such as the Contemporary Art Society is, arguably, based in their ability to form mutually useful alliances between donors, collectors and museums. If history is a guide, the future of art philanthropy is likely to be a familiar mix of serendipitous donation and strategic support, and, in the process, our public collections will continue to be both challenged and enriched.

11 Michael Harrison, 'Art and Philanthropy: T.C. Horsfall and the Manchester Art Museum', in Alan J. Kidd and K.W. Roberts (eds.), *City, Class and Culture: Studies in Social Policy and Cultural Production in Victorian Manchester,* Manchester University Press, Manchester, 1985, pp.120–47.
12 Frances Borzello, *Civilizing Caliban: The Misuse of Art,* Routledge, London, 1987; Seth Koven, 'The Whitechapel Picture Exhibition and the Politics of Seeing', in Daniel J. Sherman and Irit Rogoff (eds.), *Museum Culture: Histories, Discourse, Spectacles,* Routledge, London, 1994. pp. 22–48; Shelagh Wilson, '''The Highest Art for the Lowest People'': The Whitechapel and Other Philanthropic Art Galleries, 1877–1901', in Paul Barlow and Colin Trodd (eds.), *Governing Cultures: Art Institutions in Victorian London,* Ashgate, Farnham, 2000, pp. 172–86.
13 John House, *Impressionism for England: Samuel Courtauld as Patron and Collector,* Yale University Press, New Haven, 1994.

Helen Rees Leahy

Taking Stock
Matthew Darbyshire reflects on negotiating other people's collections

I was pondering my recent forays into various museum stores, when it suddenly occurred to me that collecting as a practice is in fact all I've ever known. This dates back to well before any invitations came from a museum to examine, edit or rearrange their archive. At the same time I also realised that a practice like mine is entirely predicated on adopting a thematic framework, so as to provide a site within which I can operate. These frameworks have always taken the form of a particular place, the objects comprising it, or the values that built it. What I'm trying to explain here is that my obsession isn't only with museums' archives or collections, but also the less premeditated collections of objects that we might encounter in, say, the home, a shop or an office. While the museum offers so much in the way of material, most artistic endeavours are far less privileged and require a much thriftier, and at times underhand, approach to amassing their components, whether via purchase, loan, replication, false pretence, or sometimes even theft.

My fascination with collections was evidenced in my art school degree show in 2005. Titled 'San Miguel', I treated the Argos catalogue as if it were a collection, and used its mass-produced Avebury furniture range as a means to reflect on my anxieties about economic globalisation and the cultural homogenisation that is a consequence of it. I hewed copies of all the furniture's profiles and fixings in order to draw attention to their designs' simultaneous suitability for a domestic, retail, corporate and museological scenario – emphasising the blurring of the distinctions between these different contexts.

My point is that this collection of glass and steel components provided the parameters within which I could explore those particular concerns, just as a museum's social history collection might in another instance. Since then my investigations have lead me to stray into other collections in wildly diverse spheres. I amassed all the bootleg renditions of the hit single 'In the air tonight' by prog-to-soft rock pioneer Phil Collins, to produce washroom Muzak in an artists' run space in east London. I exploited the lexicon of architectural faux pas of architect Will Alsop's defunct interactive museum The Public in West Bromwich to formulate an installation in London's Tate Britain. I adopted the megabrand Ralph Lauren Polo shirt to propose a new range of standardised clothing for the western world. I took a road trip surveying five of the UK's major cities as a way of amassing evidence of the infantilising Disneyfication of our public realm and created the ticket booth for the Frieze London art fair in 2010 using telecommunications giant T Mobile's kit concept store design.

It is maybe because of these very visible raids on other people's collections or repertoires that I've recently been set free in more recognised depositories. At The Collection in Lincoln for example, I was allowed to reconfigure their medieval corn

CLOCKWISE
FROM LEFT
'Showhome',
2012,
Kettle's Yard,
Cambridge, UK

'Oak Effect',
2013,
Bloomberg,
London, UK

'Stone Dump',
2013, Lincoln
Collections
Museum,
Lincoln, UK

dryer as a vitrined stone dump referencing the revered American artist Robert Smithson. At Kettle's Yard in Cambridge I was invited to reinterpret or re-ravel the founder, Jim Ede's legacy of mid twentieth century taste via contemporary bastardisations of his treasured collection.

At The Tyne and Wear Museums Trust I was granted permission to reorganise their ethnographic, archaeological and social history collections, permitting the inclusion of only handmade wooden artefacts, which I then divided according to their provenance in seven global continents and finally paired with machine-made, plastic and wood supports. At the Hepworth Wakefield I was offered the opportunity to work with William H. Ismay's collection of post-war studio ceramics. I was assisted in recreating the museum that was in fact his two-bed semi up the road from the gallery, juxtaposing his prized and patinated pots with a modern domestic quota of wipe-clean and pristine electrical white goods.

There have also been invitations from further afield, such as the one from the Galleria d'Arte Moderna (GAM) museum collection in Turin. Here I filtered down the collection to its broadest categories: the heraldic, the erotic, the abstract and the phallic, before commissioning 3D renditions of these examples, and using the latest digital software to produce polystyrene facsimiles. Polish Socialist Realist sculptor Karol Thorek's collection of stark angular plaster casts of Stalin-era heroes have been

Matthew
Darbyshire,
'The W.A. Ismay
Collection',
2013, Hepworth
Gallery,
Wakefield, UK

juxtaposed with my mirror-faceted, biomorphic and architectonic lumps that mimic the work of celebrity architects such as Zaha Hadid, Daniel Liebeskind and Frank Gehry.

But then there are other projects, involving less precious collections. For a recent public commission in Utrecht's Hoog Catharijne, a late-modern shopping complex and Ballardian nightmare, I initiated a kind of 'lesson in looking' by literally dragging together elements from around the mall to create a formal grid of nine objects that prompted reflection on where we've been, where we are and where we're going with regards to shopping in the third millennium.

Museums of course play a vital role within society, and while my practice favours patina, disorder and clutter over a regimented display of academically prescribed relics scrubbed to within an inch of their life, as long as we keep this stuff in circulation and keep on reassessing its meaning, value and connotation without prejudice or snapshot consensus we can probably rectify the aesthetic shortcomings as we go.

On the subject of museum display strategies and why I might be drawn to them: I'm of course keen to explore the politics underlying methods of acquisition, selective narratives, modes of classification and habits of display but the subversion of these conventions per se is not my primary motivation. I prefer to redirect their content to a context outside of the 'mausoleum scenario', and into a social dimension more widely relevant, such as the home, the school, the mall, the square, the surgery, or the dole office. It is these other institutions that I'm thinking of when negotiating a collection, and not just the well-meaning host that knows as well as we do that it can't ever be everything to everyone. So yes, alternatives in all areas are the impetus for my activities and while the museum's recent assumption of a more polymorphous guise

is worthy of reflection, so too is the mall, which, more alarmingly, sees itself as the cultural hub the museum once was.

With regards to the criteria for my object selections or the politics of my displays, my first point must be that I make no distinction between the two. While display is of utmost importance to me, this probably has more to do with gravity and ergonomics than any desire to legitimate or enhance something. If an object needs more than just a physical support it shouldn't be selected in the first place. I can't stand the snazzy store design solutions some flagrantly indulge in in order to do this. As we know, you can't polish a turd and so beyond the practicalities my interest in display is premised only on its ability to further totalise a work and immerse the viewer, thus increasing emotional charge and generating a more heightened bodily response. With regards to my selection of both objects and supports, I don't carry a blueprint from one work to the next, but I try to eliminate any risk of avoidable ambiguities arising. There's time for those to emerge later, and in fact I find if I try and restrain all introspective compulsions, just enough of my own dubious personal traits sneak in. It is for these reasons I gravitate towards finding the essence of what I'm thinking upfront, maybe as a way of showing my hand; or maybe it's just some twisted moral hang-up, because after all I'm never satisfied until I find my own selections a little perplexing. It's contradictory, I know, but just because we have to make our own rules doesn't mean we can't break them.

Deliberately skittish and disorderly, my object selection wants to evade classification and blur distinctions by oscillating between the high and the low, the profound and the profane, the past and the present, the singular and the stock, the substantial and the superficial, and the sublime and the silly.

With regards to arrangements, I'm pleased to say I have no recipe here either. Aren't we as artists all just putting things next to each other – whether they are sounds, images or actions? After all, tensions only arise when you put one thing next to another, and beyond addressing the threadbare question of what constitutes an art object, found or readymade entities will always struggle to transcend the sum of their parts if presented in isolation. I suppose object-arrangements appear more didactic or syntactical, because they have their own space and atmosphere, but this can still be overridden and manipulated to permit as impastoed, scrambled or cacophonic an arrangement as any other media. That's the challenge, I suppose: to wrestle and redirect what would otherwise be literal or linear. I guess I must confess here though to a formal trait that, regardless of the nature of my selections, sees me separate and group things according to formal qualities like volume, height, colour or substance. And I honestly don't know whether this levelling-out is an obsessive compulsion, a strategy to ensure a more lucid hypothesis, or a well-meant attempt to democratise and break down pre-existing hierarchies. Perhaps it is a far more cynical and reductive take on the world that suggests technology has atomised it to become nothing more than meaningless molecules and matter, devoid of nuance, and more akin to digital data and bytes.

I accept this phenomenon as part of my repertoire, and beyond this try only to impose a checklist of the basic elements of form, material, colour, scale and process. This may sound painfully traditional, but I am currently finding these core concerns to be more urgent than ever. Through scrutinising what appear to be the basic principles of sculpture I suddenly have to take stock of new materials, applications and technologies, and of course their attendant political and psychological implications. Most of us can

CLOCKWISE
FROM TOP LEFT
'IP', 2013, Hoog
Cathariine,
Utrecht, the
Netherlands

'Ideal
Standards',
2013, GAM,
Turin, Italy

'Public
Workshop',
2013, Zamek
Ujazdowski,
Warsaw,
Poland

'An Exhibition
for Modern
Living', 2011,
Hayward
Gallery,
London, UK

'Blades
House', 2007,
Gasworks,
London, UK

'Are You the
Sensitive
Type', 2014,
Herald Street,
London, UK

OPPOSITE
'Bureau', 2014,
Herald Street,
London, UK

barely fathom the composition of the physical, let alone the virtual, so it's this more hands-on and empirical approach I have recently been trying to adopt that is renewing my belief in art's true social potentials.

It feels necessary at this point to talk briefly about specialisation, or my lack of it, with regards to rummaging around museums' academically amassed collections. In homage to Robert Filliou, who writes of the artist as good-for-nothing-good-for-everything, I will stake the controversial claim that disinterestedness is key. After all, we as humans only see what we want to see and it is for this reason that I've enjoyed so much being exiled to various far-away museum stores with no prior knowledge of the collections. I'm invariably outside of my field of specialisation and therefore can only offer fresh eyes without bias, agenda or motive to persuade. This more removed glance is key for me. Not just because it's our role as artists to try and see to the crux or topple tired hierarchies, but because it's this abstract and slightly irreverent vantage point that ensures the insights necessary to excavate new meanings and establish new relationships between me, you and the stuff we're looking at.

Nothing Beautiful Unless Useful: Learning from Ancoats

Anna Colin

PREVIOUS PAGE
Humphrey
Jennings,
Spare Time,
1939, 35mm,
transferred
to DVD
15 min. Film
still courtesy
BFI National
Archive

'Nothing Beautiful Unless Useful' addresses the relationship between art and social reform between 1880 and 1940 in the industrial North West of England.[1] Mirroring the display drawn from the Contemporary Art Society's membership collections at the Whitechapel Gallery, this text focuses on the Manchester Art Museum (1886–1953), the Leeds Arts Club (1903–23) and Mass Observation (1937–49), three organisations connected by a common belief in art as a conduit for social progress. The first part of the text delves into the vision of each of these three initiatives and the circumstances around their emergence, bringing to light sometimes unexpected links between their founders, supporters, members and interlocutors. The second part acts as a guide to the exhibition's different sections: it intends to highlight the relations between form and context at play in the exhibition, as well as share some of the histories contained in the works displayed and sections represented. In that sense, the text embraces Thomas Horsfall's sociological interest in art and his compulsion for contextualisation. Furthermore, it provides a reflection on how similarly-minded artworks, cultural materials and movements, which have not been previously presented together, might relate to each other and collectively inform contemporary discourses around the agency of art.

It was the figure of Thomas Coglan Horsfall (1844–1932), encountered in the first week of my research in Manchester, who inspired the direction for 'Nothing Beautiful Unless Useful'. A philanthropist and collector who inherited his wealth from his father – a card manufacturer – and his vision from the art critic and social thinker John Ruskin, Horsfall was a quiet pioneer of modern museum culture and education. Like Ruskin and William Morris, Horsfall developed his reformist work against the backdrop of the second industrial revolution, and more specifically in response to its alienating effects. He would dedicate forty years of his life to develop and support a new type of museum for the working men and women of Manchester's inner-city district Ancoats, which had experienced the effects of rapid industrial development in the later half of the nineteenth century.

'The people who live in and near crowded towns have, it seems to me, two states to choose between – one in which beauty of many kinds shall be known and loved by the majority of the people of all classes; the other, the existing state, in which a very large number of the working classes are brutalised by their surroundings, and a very large number of the richer class live in brutalising indifference to their brutality.'[2]

Manchester Art Museum

Thomas Horsfall first started making plans for the Manchester Art Museum in 1877, gathering support from organisations including the Manchester and Salford Sanitary Association, the Ancoats Recreation Committee, the Manchester Literary Club and the Ruskin Society. Ancoats was a squalid area, filled with smoke and dwellings 'in the last stages of inhabitableness', as Friedrich Engels had first described them in 1845.[3] Thirty years on, the streets of Ancoats showed little sign of improvement. Thomas Horsfall set himself the task of ending the 'brutality' of industrial living through engaging people with art 'by means of a sensibly managed art gallery'.[4] He was driven by the firm conviction that by spreading 'knowledge and love of art and beauty',[5] art galleries could instil in the working people the 'desire and power to live rightly'.[6] Like much of his discourse on beauty, the expression 'to live rightly' is associated with religious and moralistic undertones. For right means fair, but also righteous, which is far removed from the 'indulgence of physical appetites, which would kill our higher life.'[7] Horsfall's

1 The title 'Nothing Beautiful Unless Useful' is borrowed from architect Charles Barry, who used it as a motto in his entry to the architectural competition to design Manchester Art Gallery in the 1830s.
2 Thomas Coglan Horsfall, *Art in Large Towns*, Macmillan, London, 1883, p.45.
3 Friedrich Engels, *The Condition of the Working Class in England*, Penguin, London, 2005, first published in Germany in 1845, p.97.
4 Horsfall, op.cit., p.40.
5 Ibid.
6 Thomas Coglan Horsfall, *The Study of Beauty*, Macmillan, London, 1883, p.31.
7 Ibid., p.16.

G.E. Anderton,
*Ancoats Old
Hall*, c.1900.
Courtesy of
Manchester
Libraries,
Information
and Archives,
Manchester
City Council

mission was thus both social and redemptive; as well as being a vehicle for delectation, instruction and empowerment, the future Manchester Art Museum represented a potential instrument of civic control.

The Manchester Art Museum opened its doors in 1886 in Ancoats Hall. In the lead up to its launch, the borough of Ancoats had started to benefit from the work of other left-leaning philanthropists, in particular Charles Rowley, an Ancoats-born socialist, local councillor and art dealer, and the founder of the Ancoats Recreation Committee, later renamed Ancoats Brotherhood. Charles Rowley, the self-described son of 'an early pioneer in self-education and the helping of others', first worked in local politics before turning to culture.[8]

'We got a committee together, gathered some money, and started a number of rousing things. We placed bands in the two parks in the neighbourhood; now the Corporation do it. Having got, as a result of my own election cry, baths and washhouses and a public room, we proceeded to use them profusely [...]. Our aim always has been to stimulate, to get ideas, even ideals, into practical form, and then, when more powerful bodies in command of cash take them up, we turn to something else and try fresh experiments. In 1880 we had our first exhibition of works of art. I have the very pretty illustrated catalogue now before me. Canon Barnett, of Toynbee Hall, has assured me that he has got many hints for his exhibitions in East London from our proceedings. We were at work five or six years before Toynbee Hall, but with similar ideas in our minds, stimulating, offering beautiful things, natural and artistic, giving series of University Extension lectures, by such men as Michael Sadler, Hudson Shaw, Llewelyn Smith, H. J. Mackinder, Hilaire Belloc [...].'[9]

8 Charles Rowley, *Fifty Years in Ancoats, Loss and Again*, privately published, 1899, p.5.
9 Charles Rowley, *Fifty Years Without Wages*, privately published, 1911, pp.195–98.

Anna Colin

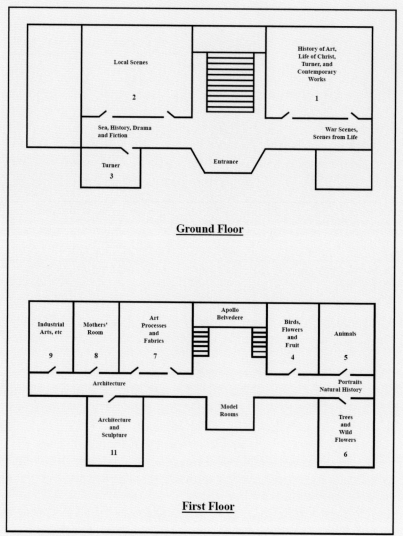

Plan of the Art Museum in late 1880s

The Ancoats Recreation Committee also started Sunday afternoon meetings with guest speakers, including Walter Crane, Ford Madox Brown and William Morris, who gave an annual lecture. Before becoming a regular of the Committee, Morris was invited by Horsfall to give a public talk on his second visit to Manchester.[10] In March 1883, Morris delivered one of his most famous and controversial speeches, 'Art, Wealth and Riches', in which he addressed the social effects of industrialisation and de-skilled labour. Causing havoc, he argued beauty and 'real art' could not be achieved through 'burdensome or degrading' work and called for the end of competitive commerce, that 'pestilential rubbish', which thrives on the exploitation of workmen.[11] Unlike Horsfall, who believed social improvement would be triggered by the instruction of art and beauty, Morris maintained 'change must come, or at least be on the way, before art can be made to touch the mass of the people.'[12] Despite their divergences, William Morris – like Charles Rowley and John Ruskin – was on the Manchester Art Museum Committee. His role was to advise with the 'Model Rooms' and the 'Art, Processes and Fabrics' galleries, which taught visitors about good and affordable design made as a result of 'intelligent' work, that is, using traditional rather than industrial means of production.

The Manchester Art Museum was split over two floors; its collection was organised according to thematic sections such as 'Local Scenes', 'Birds, Flowers and Fruits', 'Industrial

10 Edmund and Ruth Frow, *William Morris in Manchester and Salford*, Working Class Movement Library, Salford, 1996.
11 William Morris, 'Art, Wealth and Riches', lecture delivered at the Manchester Royal Institution, Mosley Street, Manchester on 6 March 1883. Available online at http://www.marxists.org/archive/morris/works/1883/riches/riches.htm [accessed 21 July 2013].
12 Ibid.

Arts', 'Animals', 'Architecture and Sculpture', and one gallery dedicated to the work of J.M.W. Turner. The collection featured oil paintings, watercolours, etchings and engravings by the Pre-Raphaelites, including William Holman Hunt, Dante Gabriel Rossetti, Edward Burne-Jones, Ford Madox Brown, Frederic J. Shields, and their contemporaries John Ruskin, Walter Crane, Emily Gertude Thomson and George Frederick Watts, as well as works by Tintoretto, Raphael and Leonardo da Vinci.

Horsfall outlined his vision for his upcoming museum in *Art and Large Towns* (1883). It would be open on Sundays – largely unusual at the time – so working people could go to the museum on their only day off. It would also be open one to two evenings a week for the same reason, and host concerts 'to induce people to come and to stay long in our museum'.[13] The collection would offer a range of art forms and objects relating to different epochs, from casts of antique sculpture to the finest examples of industrial arts, through to contemporary painting. Copies would be commissioned when necessary, for educational reasons (for use during popular lectures, for instance) or to make up for the gaps in the collection. In order to inform visitors about techniques and processes, different types of objects representing similar themes would be shown alongside each other.

> 'For example, we shall place a copy of the coloured plates of birds from Gould's *British Birds*, which have lithographed outlines, and are coloured by hand, side by side with woodcuts of the same birds from Bewick and from Yarrell, and by means of a label we shall call attention to such points as the mode in which local colour is represented in black and white, and shall invite comparison of the coloured plates and woodcuts with carefully made water-colour drawings of the same birds contained in the Art Museum.'[14]

Interpretation would be key: every artwork and object would be meticulously contextualised, explained and referenced by means of a label. Furthermore, there would be a significant social history section to engage visitors with the past and present of their locality.

Whether the Manchester Art Museum succeeded in alleviating 'the running sores of working class life in Manchester' is more than arguable.[15] If it did, it was less through art than through recreational activities.

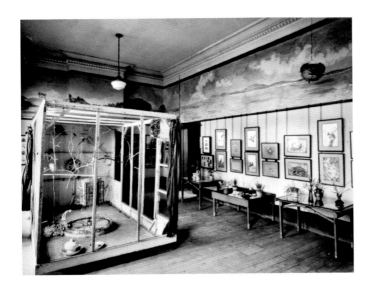

The Nature Study Room at the Art Museum in Ancoats, c.1940s. © Manchester City Galleries

13 Horsfall, *Art in Large Towns*, op.cit., p.41.
14 Ibid., p.45.
15 Ibid., p.129.

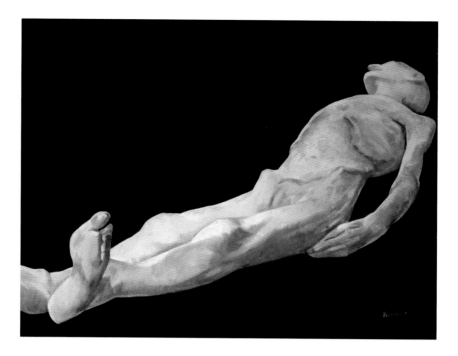

'After the initial rush, an average of 2,000 people per week visited the museum – 250 to 300 "real Ancoats people" regularly attended the Wednesday night entertainments, which consisted of music, singing, reading and recitations.'[16]

The number of evenings for popular entertainment rose from one to two a week following the first annual report, which noted that 'the mere exhibition of works of art, even with the aid of written and oral explanation, would not suffice to attract a sufficient number of visitors to the Museum to make it a force in the neighbourhood.'[17] However, in 1895 the educational aims of the museum would be reasserted following the implementation of the new Education Code. The code, which Horsfall had helped draft, stipulated that time in the museum was equivalent to school time. Alongside these new perspectives and a school's picture loan scheme, which gave a major push to children and young people's outreach, came financial trouble, neglect, more or less successful mergers, a transfer to the City in 1918 and the eventual closure of the Museum in 1953, after four decades of near-oblivion.

Despite its unfortunate ending, Manchester Art Museum remains a pioneer of museum education and a prime laboratory for the application of Ruskinian ideas into practice. A hundred and thirty years after its inception, at a time of ongoing debates on the usefulness of art, triggered as much by funders as by artists and curators, Horsfall's approach to connecting art and society is all the more relevant to revisit, and has yet to find a place in the written history of socially-oriented art.

Leeds Arts Club

In 1903, the year of the formation of the Leeds Arts Club, Michael Sadler paid tribute to Horsfall in a lecture entitled 'Undercurrents of Educational Influence. Manchester Art Museum and University Settlement'.[18] Sadler, a leading educationalist and collector of expressionist art, had the opportunity to acquaint himself with the museum and its founder, having just joined The University of Manchester as a professor. In 1911 he moved on to become Vice-Chancellor of the University of Leeds. That same year, he took up the leadership of the Leeds Arts Club, together with Frank Rutter, the newly appointed Director of Leeds Art Gallery.

16 Michael Harrison, 'Art and Philanthropy: T.C. Horsfall and the Manchester Art Museum', in Kidd and Roberts (eds.), *City, Class and Culture*, Manchester University Press, Manchester, 1985, pp.120–47, p.134.
17 Ibid., p.136.
18 Much of this section draws from Tom Steele's *Alfred Orage and the Leeds Arts Club, 1893-1923*, Orage Press, Mitcham, 2009, first published in 1990, the most detailed study of the Club to have been published to date.

A vital forum for modernist thinking and artistic experimentation, the Leeds Arts Club combined art with philosophy, radical politics, suffragism and spiritualism. When Sadler and Rutter took over, the Club had gone through several phases, the most significant of which had been under the founding leadership of writers Holbrook Jackson and Alfred Orage, the future editor of the literary magazine *The New Age*. The Club's main principles were to 'cultivate the study of ideas to induce people to think' and 'direct attention to the beautifying and uplifting power of art'.[19] Orage and Jackson drew their inspiration from Nietzsche's concept of the Superman or Overman as the creator of new values, as well as from the Fabians' policy of the 'permeation of society by new ideas rather than emphatic protest and revolt'.[20] As Tom Steele describes in his book *Alfred Orage and The Leeds Arts Club, 1893-1923* (1990), in the course of four years they made Leeds Arts Club one of the most dynamic and radical platforms for art and literary thinking outside London. In a similar vein to the Ancoats Recreation Committee, the Club organised exhibitions and music recitals, and offered weekly lectures and discussions by and with artists, writers, theosophists and social reformers, such as Charles Ginner, George Bernard Shaw, W.B. Yeats, Isabella Ford and G.K. Chesterton. The people attracted by the Club were 'the creative and educational lower-middle class', that is 'teachers, architects, journalists, typographers, illustrators, photographers, professional painters and musicians, and clergymen'.[21]

Michael Sadler and Frank Rutter's directorship marked a transition from 'late Victorian naturalist and symbolist forms' to 'abstract aesthetics'.[22] As an undergraduate, Michael Sadler had been a keen follower of Ruskin's lectures at Oxford, and later in his life he continued to embrace his master's campaign for education reform and his quest for truth and spirituality. However, he dissociated himself from Ruskin in the sense that:

> 'He failed to see that for us moderns strength and power show themselves in the great arms of traveling cranes, in the gossamer beauty of scaffolding, in the gaunt severity of Lancashire mill sheds and in the intense and silent power of dynamoes and turbines. Where there is force, there is beauty.'[23]

Sadler supported art that moved away from naturalistic representation and into the realm of the emotional and spiritual. Wassily Kandinsky, who was first brought to Michael Sadler's attention by his son, and whose book *Concerning the Spiritual in Art* (1912) he had translated, embodied both the theosophist and aesthetic ideals of the Leeds Arts Club. Sadler father and son were the first collectors and curators of his work in Britain and went to meet him in Munich on several occasions. His work became the object of numerous studies and discussions at the Club, as well as of art appreciation classes. Frank Rutter took inspiration from Kandinsky's music-inspired paintings and experiments with synesthesia, encouraging Club members to 'represent musical sound and composition by means of reflex painting, and to correlate words with drawings by representing nothing other than the emotions the words aroused.'[24]

The Leeds-based expressionist painter Jacob Kramer, a protégé of Michael Sadler, came out of that school of thought and experiment, alongside writer Herbert Read. Kramer worked on few abstract paintings: his most known one is *The Rite of Spring* (c.1920), which he is said to have completed after giving a lecture with piano accompaniment. His other works dealt with Judaism – he was a Russian Jew – and with portraiture, which he often engaged with to earn his living. He would be commissioned to paint subjects as varied as a visiting celebrity or a corpse for Leeds Medical School. Kramer

19 George Bernard Shaw quoted in Steele, op. cit., p.96.
20 Walter Crane, *An Artist's Reminiscences*, Methuen & Co, London, 1907, p.258. Available online at http://archive.org/details/anartistsremini00crangoog [accessed 21 July 2013].
21 Steele, op. cit., p.260.
22 Ibid., pp.19–20.
23 Michael Sadler, 'Reminiscences of Arnold Toynbee and Ruskin', talk given on 18 October 1913, quoted in Steele, op. cit., p.201.
24 David Thistlewood, *Herbert Read, Formless and Form*, Routledge, London, 1984, pp. 5-26 quoted in Steele, op. cit,, p.183.

William Holman Hunt, *Afternoon (Study: Sunset)*, 1883, watercolour and body colour, 17.6 x 12.6 cm. © Manchester City Galleries

James Hamilton Hay, *Wave*, c.1912–14, oil on canvas, 76.2 x 81 cm. Courtesy of Williamson Art Gallery & Museum, Birkenhead; Wirral Museums Service

would find fulfilment in the rare subjects he could build a transcendental connection with, for instance, Mahatma Ghandi, who 'filled that room with an extraordinary spiritual force',[25] or the cadaver he spent hours sketching for *Clay* (1928), which got him 'quite away from life.'[26]

Mass Observation

Modernists like Michael Sadler accompanied the rupture with the realist tradition with the late Victorians' idea that art could improve the working class. Twenty years later, as World War II was approaching and Britain's employment and export revenues were at their lowest, a new type of realism and – many have argued – of paternalism, emerged with the social research organisation Mass Observation. Like George Orwell's *The Road to Wigan Pier* (1937), Mass Observation resorted to non-scientific sociological tools to document the reality of the disempowered working classes in the decaying industrial North. The organisation issued its first statement and invited the contribution of individuals committed to social documentation through the pages of the *New Statesman*, the political and cultural magazine affiliated with the Fabian Society. Founded in 1937 by ornithologist-turned-anthropologist Tom Harrisson, poet Charles Madge and film-maker Humphrey Jennings, Mass Observation aimed to record everyday life, in particular of people whose voices were overlooked and under-represented by the government and the media of the time. In the first year, the founders established their headquarters in the industrial town of Bolton – which they designated as Worktown – carrying out large-

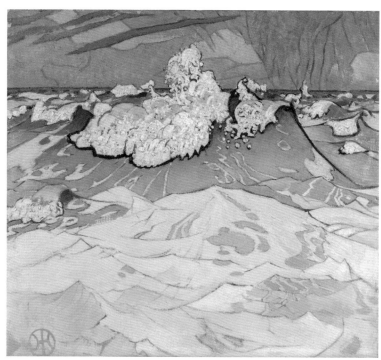

25 Jacob Kramer quoted in David Manson, *Jacob Kramer: Creativity and Loss*, Sansom and Co Ltd, Bristol, 2006, p.159.
26 Ibid., p.149.

J. Gould &
W. Hart,
*Monograph
of the
Paradiseidae;
Craspedophora
Magnifica*,
1891–98,
ink and
watercolour,
55.5 x 37 cm.
© Manchester
City Galleries

scale surveys and inviting artists to partake in this social experiment. The 'observation of the masses by the masses for the masses' involved dozens of volunteers recording their own lives and those of others, on days specified by the conductors.[27] Artists such as Julian Trevelyan, William Coldstream, Graham Bell and Humphrey Spender were brought to Bolton to contribute other forms of documentation such as sketchbooks, photographs and paintings. With Humphrey Jenning's departure from Mass Observation in 1938, artists took on a lesser role in the organisation, which would eventually turn into a form of market research that took place across the entire country. Despite being largely dismissed as non-scientific and not representative enough of working-class society, the organisation made a significant contribution to the field of modern anthropology, and the radicalism of its approach lives on. Mass Observation further set a precedent by launching, however informally, the first twentieth century town-based artists' residency scheme in the UK, a model that would become widespread in the 1970s.

A Tour of the Exhibition

Thomas Horsfall's Manchester Art Museum has not only served as a key research theme for 'Nothing Beautiful Unless Useful', but it has also inspired the selection of works and the organisation of the display. Five sections of varying sizes focus on the Manchester Art Museum, the Leeds Arts Club, Mass Observation and the socio-historical and economic context in which these three organisations emerged. The Manchester Art Museum section, the largest of the five, draws works from a range of collections including Manchester Art Gallery, to which the Horsfall Museum collection was transferred following its closure. The intention is to echo the contents and approach of Horsfall's

27 Nick Hubble, *Mass Observation and Everyday Life*, Palgrave Macmillan, New York, 2010, p.150.

Jacob Kramer,
*Abstract
Composition*,
c.1917, gouache
on paper, 29.5
x 22.5 cm.
Collection
of Leeds
Museums
and Galleries
(Leeds Art
Gallery).
Estate of John
David Roberts.
By permission
of the William
Roberts Society
/ Bridgeman
Art Library

museum in a scaled-down way. It includes works on paper that engage with beauty as an antidote to the industrial reality, such as John Ruskin's watercolours, Gertrude Emily Thomson's plant illustrations, William Holman Hunt's study *Afternoon* (1883) and James Hamilton Hay's *Wave* (c.1912–14); decorative arts, including glassware by Henry James Powell and Pilkington's Lancastrian pots; and artefacts such as a crayfish and exotic fruits sculpted in ivory, and plates from Gould's *British Birds*. Such works would have helped Horsfall in his mission to show people with limited access to nature and beauty not only what these look like but also what they could do for their social and spiritual awakening.

Composed of artworks borrowed from Leeds Art Gallery, the Leeds Arts Club section mainly includes pieces produced during Frank Rutter and Michael Sadler's era, starting with two rare abstract works from Jacob Kramer, the gouache *Abstract Composition* and the watercolour *Abstract Study*, both from 1917. Also included is his 1914 charcoal and pastel drawing titled *Industrial Landscape*. This work is again unusual in that it is one of the few that deals directly with industrial life alongside *Mining* (1921), commissioned by Sadler as the design for an unrealised mural for Leeds Town Hall. The sculptor and printmaker Eric Gill is another artist to have been commissioned by Sadler, this time for a war memorial. The print *Christ and the Money Changers* (c.1919) – an early version of the design for the stone relief that would be unveiled in 1923 – shows Christ driving businessmen out of Leeds. Gill's provocative take on the war as 'a kind of cleansing of corruption' was met with considerable criticism and is emblematic of the free thinking that Leeds Arts Club embraced.[28] The Club also supported other critical voices and practices, including those of women, when most arts clubs in Britain were still men only. One such figure was Emily Ford, who is present in the display with a portrait of Josephine Butler, the noted campaigner for women's rights, and with a study for a church mural – two works that are testament to her social and spiritual commitments. Born into a Quaker family and received into the Church of England in 1890, the Slade-educated artist spent much of her career painting frescoes and designing stain-glass windows in Anglican churches. She also co-founded the Leeds Suffrage Society, with her sister Isabella Ford, and was vice-president of the Artist Suffrage League.

The Mass Observation section focuses almost entirely on visual documentation compiled in the first year of the study of Worktown, which is kept at the Bolton Museum. A dozen photographs by Humphrey Spender, one of several Mass Observation's artists in residence, depict everyday street scenes, pub life, children at play and adults on election day, as well as Mass Observation's key figures at work in their Bolton headquarter at 85 Davenport Street. To emulate the presumed objectivity of the anthropologist, Spender endeavoured to capture situations and people's actions unnoticed, whether from a distance, in moments of confusion, or sometimes literally behind people's back. If some of Spender's images are mere snapshots of everyday situations, others are conspicuously atmospheric and evocative, such as the washing line between back-to-back rows of houses, which under his lens display quasi-animistic attributes. Spender's escape from realism finds an echo in Humphrey Jennings's *Spare Time* (1939), a film documenting the leisure activities of cotton workers in Manchester and Bolton, colliers in Pontypridd, and steelworkers in Sheffield. *Spare Time* is infused with shots and edits that let one's imagination run loose, a practice Jennings learnt from his affiliation with the surrealists.

Eric Gill, *Christ and the Money Changers*, c.1919, ink, paper, 7.4 x 8.5 cm. Collection of Leeds Museums and Galleries (Leeds Art Gallery) Photo © Tate, London 2014

28 Tom Steele, '"Us Moderns": Michael Sadler's Ancient Modernism in Education and Art'. Paper given at the Michael Sadler Centenary Conference at the University of Leeds, April 2012, unpublished.

Humphrey
Spender, *Inside
85 Davenport
Street, planning
day's activities*,
1937–38,
photograph,
43.5 x 53.5
cm, framed.
Collection of
Bolton Library
and Museum
Services ©
Bolton Council

Humphrey
Spender,
*Pub scene
– landlord
very hostile,
1937–38*,
photograph,
43.5 x 53.5
cm, framed.
Collection of
Bolton Library
and Museum
Services ©
Bolton Council

North West

When planning his museum, Thomas Horsfall recommended including a 'Local Scenes' room to equip visitors with knowledge of and pride in their local history. This approach became a standard for late-nineteenth century North West museums, which can still be found today. Taking inspiration from this model, two final sections serve to contextualise the display. Setting the scene, the first brings together industrial landscapes and representations of life and work in North West industrial centres by artists L.S. Lowry, Frank Brangwyn, Marion Rhodes and the Vorticist Edward Wadsworth. While Marion Rhodes's *Yorkshire Landscape, Looking Towards Halifax from Lindley Moor* (date unknown) shows the encroachment of industrial processes into the countryside, L.S. Lowry's *The Bandstand, Peel Park, Salford* (1931), hints, like Jennings a few years later, at the possibility of emancipation from the conditions of industrialisation through leisure and popular entertainment.

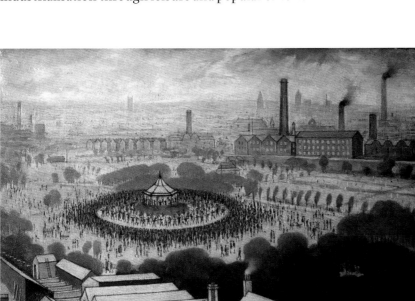

THE DEVIL ROOM

Unknown, *The Devil Room*, 1854, engraving hand-tinted with ink & watercolour, 23.8 x 54.9 cm. Lancashire Archives reference DDPR/138/87, reproduced with permission from *The Lancashire Evening Post*

OPPOSITE
Unknown, *The Cotton Lords of Preston*, c.1854, printout of ballad sheet, 42 x 29.7 cm Reproduced by kind permission of the Syndics of Cambridge University Library

The final section, titled 'The Cotton Museum', tells a short history of the cotton industry in Lancashire through artworks, objects and documents borrowed from the Harris Museum & Art Gallery and Lancashire Archives. Preston artist and suffragette Patti Mayor challenged the image of the labour-soiled and anonymous mill worker in *Half Timer* (1906), a portrait of Annie Hill, a young girl sharing her time between school and Horrockses mill. Horrockses, Preston's leading cotton manufacturer, was once directed by Thomas Miller, an art collector and the notorious instigator of the 'great Preston lock-out' (1853–54), an industrial dispute that saw mills closed to workers who demanded the restoration of decent wages. This eight-month conflict gave rise to critical cartoons and ballads, a sample of which are presented in the exhibition. Thomas Miller's collection largely disappeared and its remainders were eventually bequeathed to the Harris Museum in 2011 by one of his descendants. One of William Henry Hunt's still lives and a small portrait of Miller are exhibited as another example in the web of relations between art and industry in the nineteenth century.

When I opted for Thomas Horsfall as my anchor for the project, I learnt that he was to be the subject of a year-long display at Manchester Art Gallery. Many of the works and objects that were presented had remained boxed up and unseen since the arrival of the collection at Manchester Art Gallery sixty years earlier. Bringing Horsfall to London at the same time as the Manchester display seemed timely, and bringing him to east London, and the Whitechapel Gallery in particular, would make the influence of both his museum and of Ancoats's socio-cultural experiments come full circle. For, if Ancoats Recreation Committee's exhibitions had served as a model for Toynbee Hall's own exhibitions, the Manchester Art Museum had been acknowledged by Samuel Barnett – the founder of both Toynbee Hall and the Whitechapel Gallery – as an inspiration for the newly established gallery which opened in 1901.[29]

29 Harrison, op. cit., p.141.

THE COTTON LORDS
OF PRESTON.

Have you not heard the news of late,
About some mighty men so great,
I mean the swells of Fishergate,
    The Cotton Lords of Preston.
They are a set of stingy Blades,
They've lock'd up all their Mills and
    Shades,
So now we've nothing else to do,
But come a singing songs for you,
So with our ballads we've come out,
To tramp the country round about,
And try if we cannot live without
    The Cotton Lords of Preston.

CHORUS.

Everybody's crying shame,
On these Gentlemen by name;
Dont you think they're much to blame
    The Cotton Lords of Preston.

The working people such as we,
Pass their time in misery,
While they live in luxury,
    The Cotton Lords of Preston.
They're making money every way,
And building Factories every day,
Yet when we ask them for more pay,
They had the impudence to say,
To your demands we'll not consent,
You get enough so be content,

But we will have the Ten per Cent,
    From the Cotton Lords of Preston,
      Everybody's crying shame&c.

Our Masters say they're very sure,
That a strike we can't endure,
They all assert we're very poor.
    The Cotton Lords of Preston.
But we've determined every one,
With them we'll not be done,
For we'll not be content,
Until we get the Ten per Cent,
The Cotton Lords are sure to fall,
Both ugly, handsome, short and tall,
For we intend to conquer all,
    The Cotton Lords of Preston.
      Everybod's crying shame &c.

So men and women all of you,
Come and buy a song or two,
And assist us to subdue,
    The Cotton Lords of Preston,
We'll conquer them and no mistake,
Whatever Laws they seem to make,
And when we get the Ten per Cent,
Then we'll live happy and content,
O then we'll dance and sing with glee,
And thank you all right heartily,
When we gain the victory,
And beat the Lords of Preston.
      Everybody's crying shame &c.

Own or
Be Owned

Helen
Kaplinsky

1 James Boyle, 'The Second Enclosure Movement and the Construction of the Public Domain', in *Law and Contemporary Problems*, Vol. 66, No. 33.

2 'Common' is land owned and worked in common. Historically it provided minimum welfare for the poorest, enabling them to sustain pasturage (grazing livestock), piscary (fishing), tubury (burning turf), estover (burning or building with wood) and the right to glean after harvest. During the Saxon period, all village land was assumed to be commonly owned and worked with the exception of a few enclosed areas. Following the Norman Conquest in 1066, land was associated with a local manor and therefore owned by its lord, who bestowed rights to work the land to commoners. From the sixteenth, and throughout the seventeenth centuries, land previously granted as 'common' by landlords was gradually enclosed and put to more economically efficient use. During the eighteenth and nineteenth centuries, with the industrial revolution in full swing, enclosure became a centrally-led government policy. See Lewis Hyde, *Common as Air: Revolution, Art and Ownership*, Farrar Straus and Giroux Inc, New York, 2010, pp.28—30.

3 Miklos Rajnai and Marjorie Allthorpe-Guyton, *John Sell Cotman 1782—1842. Early Drawings in Norwich Castle Museum*, Norfolk Museum Services, Norwich, 1979, p.82.

4 William Blake, 'And did those feet in ancient time', Preface to *Milton A Poem*, c.1810.

'Damn braces: Bless relaxes' began by examining the way art schools on the East Coast of England have helped shape the local public collections of art. Artists' responses to shifts in the local landscape forced by industry appeared to me as an ongoing motif. From the nineteenth century peer-led education model of the Norwich Society of Artists, to the pioneering Time Based Media department at Humberside College in the 1980s and 1990s, students and teachers looked to their local landscape as the most immediate subject at hand. From common land to public services and digital commons, artists and their students have depicted the English landscape under threat: divided by landowners and industry in the nineteenth century, and in the 1980s and 90s, as part of the floatation on the global stock market of Britain's resources by the Thatcher Government.

The early Internet was considered comparable to the physical common landscape; a digital common where self-appointed rights entitled the user to consider any material they came across as up for grabs. While common peasants had been bestowed with the right to collect firewood, an online user might assume the right to click and download an image to their desktop. Today, in what has been termed 'the second enclosure', legislative fences have been erected to protect intellectual property online and curb the permissive culture of freely sharing information.[1] The artist in both eras is positioned as the quintessential libertarian romantic, seeking to banish control over territories on- and offline. Landscapes are coded, their symbolic and actual ownership traced by walls and paths. The contestation of liberty and anti-establishment politics in response to three layers of privatisation that can be identified forms the basis for the display. From a peasant rebellion against enclosure of common land in the sixteenth century, via William Blake, who lived through the age of the French Revolution, to today's battle for the digital liberal economy, the artists whose work has been selected sympathise with subjects who lose their rights and freedoms as a result of enclosure.

I began by looking at the Norwich Society of Artists. Founded in 1803 as a peer-learning, self-taught group, the Society was a precursor to the establishment of the Norwich School of Design in 1845, which evolved into the current Norwich University of the Arts. Its members took the local landscape as the focus of their studies, and one site of repeated visitation was Mousehold Heath, an area of 'common' land just outside the city of Norwich.[2] The Norwich Castle Museum and Art Gallery, which holds a significant collection of works by Society artists, was first on my list of research visits. In search of an English Romanticism, the work to capture my attention was *Kett's Castle, Norwich* (c. 1809–10) by John Sell Cotman, who became president of the Society in 1811. Kett's Castle is the romantic local name for the ruins of St. Michael's Chapel on Mousehold Heath, renamed following its role as the headquarters for Kett's rebellion of 1549. Led by landowner Robert Kett, 16,000 dispossessed peasants fought against the 'enclosure' of Mousehold. Enclosure saw private landowners erect fences to delineate property on previously commonly owned and worked land. The motivation for enclosure was to generate a greater profit from the land through increasingly efficient farming methods and mining. Cotman depicts the nineteenth century ruined chapel as an enigmatic 'weird silhouette', set atop blocks of flat colour, designating the different uses of the land.[3] The territory is cut across diagonally, with the hedge specifying enclosure. The scrubland around the ruin is a murky green, while the newly cultivated land has an ochre and reddish hue. The story of Kett's rebellion and the depiction of Mousehold by the Society artists provided me with an insight into the contested nature of the seemingly safe 'green and pleasant' English landscape.[4] What to a twenty-first century observer is a conservative and genteel vision of the English common peasant

John Sell
Cotman,
*Kett's Castle,
Norwich,*
c.1809–10,
pencil and
watercolour
drawing.
Courtesy
Norfolk
Museums
Service
(Norwich
Castle
Museum &
Art Gallery)

is actually an image loaded with political tension. What might at first be construed as a nostalgic view of the peasant, working or resting in an open field, in fact attests to the disappearing rights of the commoners to access land following enclosure.

Suppressed by mercenaries, the rebels of 1549 were defeated, Kett was imprisoned at the Tower of London and later hung from the gallows at Norwich Castle. Today Norwich Castle Museum bears a plaque dedicated to Robert Kett, commemorating him as a 'COURAGEOUS LEADER IN THE LONG STRUGGLE OF THE COMMON PEOPLE OF ENGLAND TO ESCAPE FROM A SERVILE LIFE INTO THE FREEDOM OF JUST CONDITIONS'. Kett's story was mythologised not only through the picturesque landscape of the nineteenth century, but also through radical politics in the twentieth. The memorial plaque was initiated by Alderman Fred Henderson (c. 1885–1957), a Labour Party politician and in 1939–40 Lord Mayor of the City of Norwich. Aged 19, as a founding member of the Socialist League in Norwich, Henderson was imprisoned in Norwich Castle Jail (today the Museum) for inciting food riots, which saw disgruntled and politicised unemployed people looting food. The plaque immortalises Kett as a hero who fought for access to common usage of land by the citizens of Norwich, drawing on the history of the rebellion as a precedent through which to read the struggle of the labouring classes during the twentieth century. The value we attribute to the English landscape and the posthumous elevation of Kett from enemy of the state to hero of the people, can be credited to John Sell Cotman and his contemporaries, who made the common heaths and scrublands their subject.

The Heath was popular for recreation and Cotman is said to have had fond memories of playing there as a boy. He was born in 1782, and significant enclosure of Mousehold began in 1790, so he would have only just remembered the open Heath. Revisiting it as an adult the addition of hedges would have been striking. Cotman depicts the Mousehold of his childhood; an open vista of rolling hills and winding paths carved through centuries of freedom to wander through the landscape. The figures in Mousehold Heath provide an agency associated with leisure rather than labour, the sentimental tableau reflecting

John Sell Cotman, *Mousehold Heath*, c.1835–42, pencil and watercolour drawing. Courtesy Norfolk Museums Service (Norwich Castle Museum & Art Gallery)

'special significance... inspired by Cotman's deep attachment to his native Norfolk'.[5] This attachment to Norwich was shared by Jeremiah James Colman MP (1830–98), the founder of Colman's , the famous mustard manufacturer . In 1898 Colman bequeathed 20 Norwich School paintings to the Norwich Museum. His son Russell James Colman (1861–1946) bequeathed more than 3,000 works in 1946, and supported the establishment of a gallery within Norwich Castle Museum to house the collection, which opened in 1951. For the exhibition at the Whitechapel Gallery and Middlesbrough Institute of Modern Art (mima) the pictures had to be displayed as facsimiles: according to the terms of the bequest they are not allowed to leave Norwich Castle Museum and Gallery. Here it is not the author, but the owner of the property – in this case an artwork – who posthumously defines access.

Cotman, although born and based in Norwich for a large portion of his career, first studied in London under physician Dr. Thomas Monro, who was also a patron to Peter DeWint and J.M.W. Turner. Monro's residence at Adelphi Terrace, London, was an 'informal academy' for the fraternity of landscape artists, which, alongside the Norwich Society, was a model that preceded State art education.[6] As a promoter of art education, Cotman kept a library of more than 1,000 drawings, which he loaned to students. This Circulating Collection, or Circulating Portfolio, enabled local amateurs to subscribe and study his technique.[7] Providing a similar function for the amateur artist, Turner's

5 Rainai and Allthorpe-Guyton, op. cit., p.85.
6 'Poetry of Place', Usher Gallery Lincoln, Lincoln County Council, Lincoln, 1997, p.42.
7 David Hill, *Cotman in the North: Watercolours of Durham and Yorkshire*, Yale University Press, New Haven, 2005, p.161.

Liber Studorium (1807–19) or 'Book of Studies', included 71 of an intended 100 landscape etchings and engravings in the categories Historical, Pastoral and Marine. It is likely that the print *After Turner* in the collection at Gainsborough Old Hall, Lincolnshire, was done by a student of Turner's, as it bears an unmistakable resemblance to one of the prints from his publication, *Solway Moss* (1816). Solway Moss, mostly rough, uncultivated bogland, was known as 'The Debateable Land'. A buffer between England and Scotland, it was the site of a battle between Henry VIII and James V of Scotland in 1542. The year after Turner's imagining of the savage ancient landscape saw the building of the Turnpike Road through Solway Moss, and enclosure transformed the scrubland soon after.[8]

More than 150 years after Turner sketched 'The Debateable Land', artist Fran Cottell invited women from all walks of life to join her for a 'meeting' on this same territory, today the Northumberland National Park. The large-scale public performance, *A Meeting Outside Time* (1988) brought together more than thirty local women, described by Cottell as collaborators, through an open-call newspaper advert. The women travelled by coach from Newcastle and were split into groups and dropped at intervals across the landscape cut through by Hadrian's Wall – the frontier of the Roman Empire. Approaching from various routes, the women reconvened at an open moorland site, which Cottell understood as 'neutral' territory. At this point they performed a 'symbolic casting off of everyday pre-occupations by leaving personal markers – objects, written words'.[9] Although the exact nature of these personal markers is restricted to the private exchanges between the women, Cottell recorded interviews with each collaborator after the event. Their words highlight the value of sharing time on this day, as an antidote to a sense of isolation. With the loss of common assets via privatisation, British society became increasingly atomised, relying on individualised responsibility.

Earlier that year, Fran Cottell took up the post of Time Based artist in residence at Humberside College, in Kingston upon Hull. Time Based Media was not a course in itself, but a department students from any fine art discipline could opt into, often in order to test a collaborative, experimental approach in a public space. The project resulting from Cottell's residency – *The Blue Line* (1988) – saw students develop eleven live art responses to the landscape, emphasising the role of the waterway in city life. Over the course of 12 hours, these responses were woven through the city with a bus called The Blue Line, transporting an estimated audience of 5,000 from one performance to the next. *Blue Bondage Line*, a performance by Silvy Szulman, a star student of the Time Based department, mirrored the industry of the Humber as a goods distribution port by tying her possessions along a rope and dragging them on her hands and knees through the city centre on a busy shopping day. Tim Brennan, with fellow student Mark Hudson, staged a funeral procession for people who used to work in the Hull fishing industry. As a curator and artist, Brennan's practice continues his interest, developed as a student, of producing guided walks that reflect on public histories of landscape.

After working with the students on *The Blue Line,* Cottell was commissioned by Hull Time Based Arts to produce the installation and performance *Source*, which she undertook in collaboration with Jan Howarth. The 'multi-media journey into the world of water' addressed the issue of privatisation of resources, pointing to 'the paradox of bottled water; by drawing comparisons with the interdependant circulatory systems of humans, whose bodies are 90–50% water and those of the wider environment from the wash basin to the sea'.[10] Perrier mineral water bottles, standing in lines and resembling skittles, or perhaps stand ins for their own bodies, were projected into the gallery

8 English Heritage, *English Heritage Battlefield Report: Solway Moss 1542*, 1995, available online at http://www.english-heritage.org.uk/content/imported-docs/p-t/solway.pdf.
9 Information sheet produced by Projects UK, for those interested in participating in *A Meeting Outside Time.*
10 Fran Cottell and Jan Howarth, Press release *Source*, 1988. Commissioned for Hull Time Based Arts and Posterngate Gallery, Hull, and later that same year re-worked for Chisenhale Gallery, London.

alongside images and recordings of the East Coast. Bottled water – the commodification of a natural resource – which can do little in terms of product to define itself from competitors, is driven by marketing. Perrier were the first to create desirability around their brand; the sheen of a chic yuppie lifestyle pushed sales from 12 million bottles in 1980 to 152 million a decade later.[11] Individuals buying into bottled water represented a microcosm of the wider shift in the management of resources in this period. In 1989, Thames Water was privatised as Thames Water Utilities Limited, and listed on the London Stock Exchange.

Part commissioning organisation, part collective, Hull Time Based Arts (HTBA, 1984–2002) opposed the opening up of these new markets.[12] They commissioned work that played out a punkish attitude, resolutely outside the art market, both in the time based, ephemeral nature of the work and the politics. Many credit the geographically isolated location of Kingston upon Hull for providing this perceived space 'outside' the market. Mike Stubbs, who went on to become the director of HTBA (1988–2002) first arrived in Hull on a residency at the Ferens Art Gallery in 1987. He produced an ambitious installation and performance, a collision of identity and technology, entitled *Fragility of Things.* Stubbs recounts the excitement and effort of wynching a crashed car into the foyer of the Ferens, beside which he traced the contours of his body, corpse-like on the gallery floor. The legacy of HTBA is imprinted on the Ferens Art Gallery, offering the first Live Art museum space in the UK, and a focus for the collection of new media art that continues today. The artists who taught Time Based Media at Humberside College – including Rob Gawthrop and Gillian Dyson – were also

11 Hamo Forsyth, 'Bottled water has become liquid gold', *The Money Programme*, BBC News Business, 23 November 2010.
12 The HTBA archive has recently entered the Bristol University Live Art Archive. Other archive material has been loaned directly from the artists.

Helen Kaplinsky

Peter DeWint, *Lincolnshire Landscape (Near Horncastle)*, c.1813–26, oil on canvas, 107 x 171 cm. Courtesy The Collection: Art and Archaeology in Lincolnshire (Usher Gallery, Lincoln)

key figures in the running of HTBA. Students often became involved in HTBA's annual ROOT Festival and were encouraged to initiate activity without prior permission, take over municipal space, self-organise and work collectively. The performance *Monument*, directed by Man Act, opened the 1989 ROOT festival.[13]

The week-long workshop involved smashing rocks on the paving stones of the town square in Hull outside the Ferens Art Gallery. Staged on the bicentenary of the French Revolution, this countercultural project mirrored the anti-establishment ethos of William Blake and referred to prior co-produced art movements, and particularly the Situationists' slogan of the May 1968 protests – *Under the paving stones, the beach*.

The title of the exhibition 'Damn braces: Bless relaxes' is taken from William Blake's *Proverbs of Hell*, which was written in 1789, the same year the storming of the Bastille in Paris took place. The violence evoked in Blake's *The Marriage of Heaven and Hell*, of which the 'Proverbs' are one part, is a response to the chaos of the American Revolution (1775–83) and closer to home to the revolution in France. Blake's poetry was a political tool and the *braces* he condemns are the institutions of his time he railed against – the slave trade and the empire. The liberal ethics Blake chose instead, including free love, equality and imagination, are echoed in the countercultural ethic of HTBA from the late 1980s, as well as the Free Software movement in the early 2000s. In 2001 software giant IBM launched the Peace, Love and Linux campaign in San Francisco that used public space to promote software through a guerrilla graffiti campaign. As early as 1977, Free Software campaigner Richard Stallman had a badge designed at a DIY stall at a science-fiction fair, for which he came up with the slogan 'Impeach God'.[14] Putting God on trial was not just an atheist stab at the authority

13 Man Act consisted of Simon Thorne and Phillip Mackenzie. They created live art works examining the construction of masculinity.

14 Sam Williams, *Free as in Freedom*, Oreilly Online Catalogue, March 2002, available on http://oreilly.com/openbook/freedom/ch04.html.

LOCAL NEWS

SHARES FOR ALL: Simon Poulter with his glossy prospectuses...but the couple above seemed a little doubtful about his offer

TWO ambitious new art works highlighting opposite ends of the marketing world were launched in Hull this week.

One features the flotation of a spoof company planning to privatise heritage sites, including Stonehenge and Windsor Castle. The other will see fly posters cover an empty city centre building in a campaign linked to a global computer network.

Both works have been commissioned by Hull Time Based Arts as part of its new two-week programme, called Propaganda ? Simon Poulter's UK Ltd will be officially floated today at the Ferens Art Gallery after giving away millions of "shares" to the public. He has used a glossy share prospectus to parody privatisation and has opened share shops around the country in the build-up to the flotation.

"One of the central features of the piece has been to expose inconsistencies in the way public

Getting to the art of privatisation...

By Angus Young
NEWS REPORTER

utility privatisation has been handled," said Mr Poulter, UK Ltd's self-styled chief executive officer. "Each step has contained a 'sting' – the prospectuses look and feel like the real thing but when you open them they expose privatisation failures. The Press releases purport to offer shares in everything but there are no shares," he added.

In contrast, Katherine Moonan's Prime Site will plaster fly posters over the front of the former ABC cinema in Ferensway.

The images will also be displayed on the bulletin board of the Internet information exchange network, which links computer users around the world.

"Prime Site is essentially DIY propaganda campaign," she said. "The work uses fly posting as its medium because it is cheap, highly localised and constantly in a state of flux."

The programme also includes a discussion afternoon at the Ferens tomorrow when the Bishop of Hull, the Rt Rev James Jones, will be among speakers on the themes of resolution, truth and lies.

Hull Screen is also presenting a short season of propaganda films from Britain, America, Nazi Germany and Russia.

Simon Poulter, *UK Ltd* (Part of Propaganda Series), Press clipping, *Hull Daily Mail,* 3 March 1995. Courtesy University of Bristol Theatre Collection. © Simon Poulter

Certificate of Share Ownership No 4789/1147

One Hundred & Fifty Million Shares

150,000,000

The Bearer of this certificate is cordially invited to validate it at the UK Ltd Official Flotation at 6.30pm on 3rd March 1995 at the Ferens Art Gallery, Hull. Prompt attendance is advisable.

UK Ltd 0% INTEREST SHARE OFFER

Dated this Third Day of March Nineteen Hundred and Ninety Five

1995

Issued under UK complete sell off guidelines
You are advised that deregulated shares can increase dramatically in value

Issued at 8 Posterngate, Hull

Invalid without approved seal

of the Church in America, in the context of the Watergate scandal of the 1970s it represented a mistrust of all given authority, including 'democratically' elected governance. The historical roots of the liberal sentiments behind Stallman's motto 'Free as in Freedom' can be traced back to Blake's slogan – 'Damn braces: Bless relaxes': a moral code at odds with the centralised power of Church and State.[15]

In his book *The Net Effect: Romanticism, Capitalism and the Internet*, Thomas Streeter describes how figures such as web pioneer Ted Nelson, and editor of *Whole Earth Catalog* Stewart Brand popularised a romantic, individualist representation of computing, which in turn resulted in a new lease of life for neo-liberalism. Streeter draws a direct line between Ted Nelson and William Blake as romantic rebel heroes.[16] Both revel in a visionary and polemical turn of phrase. Blake's poem *Proverbs of Hell* (c.1793), was a liberal call to arms. Falling somewhere between the artistic visionary and the visionary entrepreneur, was an intermingling of two worlds that artist Simon Poulter recognised in his 'media manipulation' strategy employed for two commissions for HTBA: *Propaganda* (1995) and *Counter Marketing* (1996). Both included a process of observation and reflection, exploiting the role of imagination and desire in the production of private ownership. *Propaganda* considered government marketing at the end of the Tory privatisation years (loosely 1981-1991 under Chancellor Nigel Lawson), appropriating the tactics and rhetoric of their aggressive marketing campaign. Poulter and Stubbs peddled a number of stories in the media, featuring Poulter's fake company UK Ltd's plans to privatise Stonehenge. Poulter mimicked government tactics, producing around

15 The full quote of Stallman from which this motto comes is: 'Free software is software that respects your freedom and the social solidarity of your community. So it's free as in freedom.' Tim Fergerson, 'Stallman: Free Software Battling for Hearts and Minds', ZDNet, 6 April 2011, available online at http://www.zdnet.com/stallman-free-software-battling-for-hearts-and-minds-3040154205/.

16 Thomas Streeter, *The Net Effect: Romanticism, Capitalism and the Internet*, New York University Press, New York and London, 2011, pp. 61–63.

2,000 mock pathfinder prospectuses, selling shares in a Stonehenge theme park. For *Counter Marketing* Poulter employed pithy slogans that hark back to Blake's rebel hero figure. For a poster displayed outside the offices of the New Economics Foundation think tank (founded in 1986) the artist revised Che Guevara's phrase 'Be realistic – Demand the Impossible' to 'Be realistic – Market the Impossible'. This parody of the original phrase points to a dispossession of political imagination.

Blake advocated imagination as a political force. The stories behind the nineteenth century landscape painting in this exhibition, far from imitating nature, might be seen as political demands for a territory without borders. Rather than presenting an accurate, topographical representation of the landscape, the artists asserted their sympathies for the rights of the disappearing English peasant. *Lincolnshire Landscape (Near Horncastle)* (c.1813-26) is an act of political imagination. DeWint inserts gleaners (the poorest of peasants gathering the remains of a crop) into his harvest scene. At the time this work was painted, after the enclosures, these peasants would have been trespassing in this area of Lincolnshire landscape.[17] Despite experiencing the creeping enclosure of Mousehold Heath, Cotman eliminated the hedges that indicate boundaries of private land in order to paint the relatively open Heath of his childhood. The collective, time-based 'actions' of HTBA took place in the shadow of the fall of the Berlin Wall. These structural shifts in property and territory are events in time, and the work produced by HTBA was specifically time-based and produced by artists who were also political activists. Artist, activist and director Mike Stubbs framed the aims of HTBA thus: 'With all this talk of walls falling, boundaries breaking and free trading, it is sickening to see the rise of fascism across Europe. Until internal perceptive boundaries change along with the physical ones, xenophobia will persist.'[18]

In 1996, artist and activist Heath Bunting (alongside artists Daniel García Andújar, Rachel Baker and Minerva Cuevas) set up the online group irational.org to provide pragmatic strategies for the last remaining space left in public ownership with the realisation that 'Life's harder than it used to be... in the post-Thatcher Britain of 1996'.[19] The site was used by him and other artists to facilitate the crossing of physical borders through online activity, 'finding and documenting ways of crossing borders without needing a passport, without requiring the states on either side of a line'.[20] Irational.org monitors institutions in order to find the cracks in their apparently tight security seals, 'gateways' as Bunting refers to them, points of entry to enable a re-visioning of a propertied landscape.[21]

DeWint made many paintings of the West Fen in Lincolnshire, a water-logged heath that was used for grazing and harvesting reed for thatching, prior to the drainage and re-routing of streams, which enabled crop rotation and increasingly mechanised agriculture. The original Enclosure Acts criminalised common people, turning them from 'decent husbandmen into a mob of beggars and thieves'.[22] Billy Purvis (1784–1853), a Geordie clown and local celebrity would perform his sketch 'stealing the bundle' at agricultural fairs, acting out the absurdity of the nuisance of commoners who were criminalised for collecting firewood and gleaning on previously common land. This satirical act, recorded in popular prints and paintings at the time, has an analogue in the late twentieth century with Heath Bunting's *Skint – The Internet Beggar* (1996) . This was the artist's first commission and an invitation from HTBA's Mike Stubbs. The project was a form for online credit-card transfers As a member of the property-less, disempowered underclass of Thatcher's Britain, Bunting borrowed the archaic language of the abject Victorian beggar – 'Excuse me mister! Could you spare

Simon Poulter, *UK Ltd* (Part of Propaganda Series) Privatise Stonehenge Share Offer, 1995. Courtesy of University of Bristol Theatre Collection © Simon Poulter

17 Ian Waites, *Common Land in English Painting 1700-1850*, The Boydell Press, Woodbridge, 2012, p.64.
18 Mike Stubbs, *ROOT '92*,VHS, Hull Time Based Arts, 1992.
19 Inke Arnes, *The Hartware Guide to Irational*, Revolver, Frankfurt, p.49.
20 Matthew Fuller, 'The Expressiveness of Insubordination' in *The Hartware Guide to Irational*, p.5.
21 Fuller, op. cit., p.9.
22 Boyle, op. cit., p.35.

me a dollar?' – with the beggar returning the thanks of 'God bless you sir', to confirm receipt of credit-card details. Bunting proceeded to hack this plea into the guestbook page of corporate websites, which resulted in a bounty of several thousand dollars.[23] Bunting had made work offline before going online, and his pursuits in urban exploration amounted to research for the online proposals. He spent most of the early 1990s 'wandering the streets... doing graffiti and looking in trash', and sketches the well-worn image of the Situationist *dérive*, romantic in the sense of freely roaming outside the given strictures of the economy.[24]

Rachel Greene contextualises Bunting and fellow net.art[25] artist Alexi Shulgin's engagement with domains within a colonial North American history, saying 'Like land titles in uncharted territories, in the mid-1990s domain names were entirely up for grabs'.[26] In fact the colonisation of the Internet did not wrongly assume an uncharted territory and require the suppression of a native people. Perhaps it is more comparable to the shifts in landownership in England, whereby 'common' public territory was eroded through the interests of a liberal economy and government legislation. The insidious piecemeal nature of privatisation can be held up as a parallel, whereby economic growth and the entrepreneurial attitude of individuals – first farmers working the land hoping to gain better yield and secondly a generation of dotcom speculators investing in the virtual market – are complicit in producing the private space. The work *_readme. html (Own, Be Owned or Remain Invisible)* (1998) by Heath Bunting addresses the terms of ownership in the Internet. It includes the artist appropriating an article about himself, originally written for the *Daily Telegraph* and republishing it on irational.org, with a hyperlink attached to most words. One (www.one.com) is (www.is.com) made (www.made.com) etc... aware of which domains are and are not owned by whether the hyperlink for that particular word is registered, and by clicking on them you end up visiting a commercial website or a virtual dead-end. Grey text turns black when the link has been visited. The artist's own name, as well as the words 'mother' 'creates' 'disbelief' 'Backspace' and others apparently associated with his identity are not hyperlinked.[27] This work is often cited as emblematic in its discussion of identity politics and its visibility online at a particular moment in the history of the Internet. Just as the circulation of identity became key to the monetisation of the Internet with *_readme.html,*

23 Rachel Greene, *Internet Art*, 2004, Thames and Hudson, London, p.35.

24 Arnes, op.cit., p.36.

25 The term 'net.art' is most often cited as first having been coined by Vuk Ćosić (born Belgrade, 1966) in 1995. The term came to him through an anonymous email, which included a stream of text glitches amid which jumped out 'net.art'. It proliferated as a term through discussions between artists, activists, intellectuals and technologists who produced content and commentary around Internet Art through mailing lists, websites and BBS (Bulletin Board System), including Nettime, irational.org and bbs.thing.net. The term is defined on various grounds as medium (browser-based projects, a low-tech aesthetic of visible coding and hyperlinks), art historically (1993/94—early 2000s in parallel with the collapse of the dotcom bubble) and a specific group of artists who are profiled in Greene, op. cit., pp. 14—28.

26 Greene, op. cit., p.42.

27 Backspace was an Internet culture members' space, established by Bunting and James Stevens, among others, which existed between 1996 and 1999. The website backspace.org, which is still live, is a fantastic work that reflects the tidal locality of Backspace next to the Thames.

Bunting asserts he will not allow his identity to become commercial property.

The relationship in digital culture between the 'free market' and 'free expression' was imprinted early on by the Free Software movement. The argument for a digital commons distinguishes between material and intellectual property; 'information wants to be free' because it can be copied without the owner being excluded from benefit, as opposed to material that is naturally wedded to property, because it is used up when disseminated.[28] Digital commons have come under criticism for their complicity with a liberal imperative, benefiting the owner who accumulates intellectual property from the user group while defending the exclusion of the needy when it comes to material property. The digital market, like the market for prints in Turner's age, has been a transformational educational tool enabling the development of ideas by increasing the flow of information. While Cotman's Circulating Library was restricted to lending his individual drawings to a small community of Norwich Society artists, Turner's *Liber Studiorium* was in print form, a multiple publication. Turner and Cotman both placed examples of their work in free circulation where they could become 'memes' within the English landscape-painting vernacular.

28 'Free Property: on Social Criticism in the Form of Software Licence' in *On Wikileaks, Bitcoin, Copyleft Three Critiques of Hacktivism*, The Wine and Cheese Appreciation Society of Greater London and Kittens Editorial Collective, 2013, p.34.

Skint - The Internet Beggar

lurking in piss and puke stinking alleys of the info supa high way
squating almost invisibly in piles of corporate data trash
the internet beggar only concerned with his own addictions
tries to blag a dollar off disgusted passers by

>Excuse me mister !
>could you spare a dollar ?

ok you humble internet beggar
charge my:

VISA   MasterCard

credit card number: [   ]   expiration date: [   ]

name as printed on card: [   ]

amount $ [   ]

  there you go mate

>god bless you sir !

Artist Oliver Laric enacts his interest in free access and dissemination of intellectual property online, inspired by Free Software activism and Internet memes. With a 3D scanner he is imaging objects in The Usher and Lincoln Collection as part of an ambitious Contemporary Art Society commission to make facsimiles of objects accessible and distributable online. The copy produced through this process can be played out in both digital and sculptural domains by a 'prosumer' (producing and consuming) audience. The Usher Collection is founded on the collection of Lincoln-born businessman and jeweller James Ward Usher (1845–1921) who bequeathed his collection and funds to build a gallery to house it to the city of Lincoln. A keen collector of ceramics, clocks and watches, coins, silver, enamels and miniatures, Usher acquired his fortune through his ownership over the rights to the 'the Lincoln Imp', a figure from Lincoln Cathedral. Usher sold the image of the imp on a variety of products, from jewellery to cutlery. While the existence and quality of the collection was built upon wealth accumulated through owning rights to intellectual property, Laric acts without regard for such licenses. Rather than licensing his 3D scan copies under 'creative commons', a license which borrows its name from the 'common' ownership laws of English land, the artist has opted to work outside the law and licensing altogether.[29]

For Kett's rebels, freedom was a right to occupy and work shared land in Norfolk, Blake sought freedom from the imposition of the establishment, while today's artists seek rights to share information freely and freedom from surveillance and the legal barriers around intellectual property. In the Old Testament *Book of Job* God allows Satan to withdraw the material wealth of Job in order to test his faith. The story has been a fulcrum for believers questioning why the righteous suffer. William Blake's illustration of the story 'Behold now Behemoth which I made with thee' depicts God explaining his creation of the material world, represented by two creatures, the hippopotamus,

29 The plans for the printing of the collection will be distributed online via lincoln3dscans.co.uk according to the ethics of free and open use.

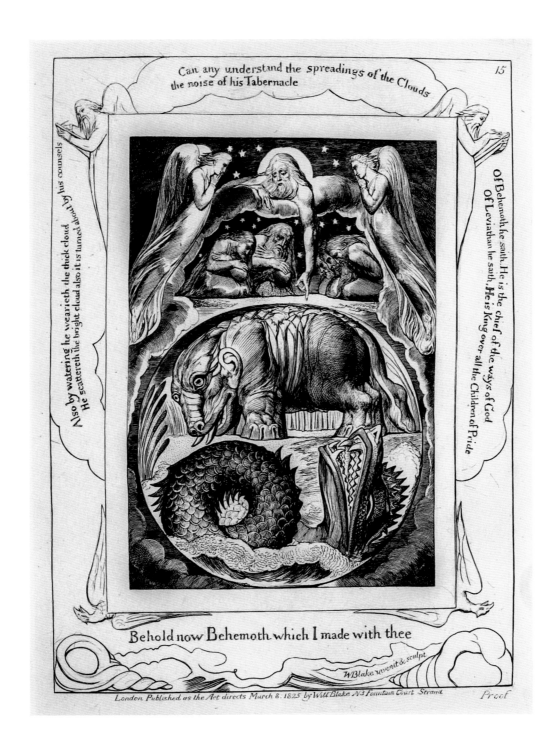

East Coast

Behemoth (the animal kingdom and land) and the snake, Leviathan (sea life). Job is made to experience the value of material wealth, property and ownership through denial. This fable extends to discussions today concerning the information economy. Looking back across three centuries of responses to the landscape, artists have sought to banish private ownership over territories on- and off-line. The story of the common, from the landscape to the digital realm, highlights an ambiguity in perception of what is held in common. The narrative thread only becomes clear at the point of withdrawal – the English landscape was only temporarily bequeathed to common peasants, while the Internet, despite appearing to early users as a digital common, was in fact always up for grabs, to be monetised and controlled by commercial interests. Like the artists before him, Laric defends the righ of the disavowed commoner by reminding us of what we stand to lose.

OPPOSITE
Oliver Laric,
The Lincoln 3D Scans Project,
2013. lincoln3d
scans.co.uk/
gallery/

Oliver Laric,
The Lincoln 3D Scans Project,
2013, wallpaper.
Installation
view,
Whitechapel
Gallery. Photo:
Stephen White

The Best
Is Not
Too Good
For You

Ingrid
Swenson

Value is an oxymoron of a word. Jekyll and Hyde-like it embodies seemingly conflicting positions and flip-flops between the two, while at times apparently straddling both. When it is used in terms of a monetary transaction in the context of market forces it refers to something that is extrinsic and definable – price. Equally, however, value can be used to define an intrinsically held principle, opinion or belief that is incalculable, such as democracy or freedom. Oscar Wilde acknowledged this conundrum when he described a cynic as someone 'who knows the price of everything and the value of nothing'. He understood the inherent dichotomy of human desire, which lies at the very heart of both these distinct and contrasting versions of value. On the one hand there is the drive to achieve material wealth as a route to happiness, and on the other, the ambition to strip away our vulgar obsession with worldly things seems to provide a structure for us to prosper in a more humanitarian or spiritual way.

Art occupies an immensely complex position in relation to these two divergent, even contradictory, understandings of value. It is a widely held view that the greatest art succeeds by transcending its base materiality. Yet it is also held that those who are able to appreciate these great works are the privileged few, who have written the rulebook on what success looks like, identifying what does or does not qualify as the best. It follows therefore that art's intrinsic value – what makes it authentic, unique and exquisite – is defined and assessed by a cultural elite. And this valued art can then be acquired by an economic elite, for whom the higher the price the better. While one could argue that this is largely still the case (as the consistently robust auction and primary market prices in the midst of a deep recession would indicate), both historically and currently there are a number of challenges to this view that suggest different narratives. Walter Benjamin's *The Work of Art in the Age of Mechanical Reproduction* (1936) proposed a Marxist reading of art's authenticity and thus value in the context of mass image-making, particularly film and photography. With the backdrop of rising fascism in Europe – and particularly in his native Germany – Benjamin's text was written in an effort to describe a theory of art that would be 'useful for the formulation of revolutionary demands in the politics of art'.[1]

The English critic John Berger picked up on Benjamin's assessment of the impact of mechanical reproduction in his own Marxist critique, *Ways of Seeing*, which was both a publication and a four-part television series watched by mass audiences in 1972. Berger used television as a way of reinforcing his argument, broadcasting it into sitting rooms throughout the country. He proposed that the modern means of production had eradicated art's authoritative position and 'For the first time ever, images of art have become ephemeral, ubiquitous, insubstantial, available, valueless, free.'[2] So for Berger, to be without value is not an indication of impoverishment, but in fact the opposite – liberation. From this perspective, art can take root everywhere and for everyone, and have a part to play in daily life.

Benjamin's views are also echoed in the ideas of another English critic, Lawrence Alloway, whose position is particularly pertinent, because he not only advocated the dissemination of art (high culture) to the masses via modern means of communication, but further, he proposed that 'culture is what society does.' In his 1959 clarion call, 'The Long Front of Culture', he stated:

'The abundance of Twentieth Century communication is an embarrassment to the traditionally educated custodian of culture. The aesthetics of plenty oppose a very strong tradition which dramatises the arts as the possession of an elite. These "keepers of the flame" master a central (not too large)

1 Preface to *The Work of Art in the Age of Mechanical Reproduction*, 1936. H. Arendt (ed.), Walter Benjamin, *Illuminations,* Fontana Press, London, 1973.
2 John Berger, *Ways of Seeing*, Penguin, London, 1977, p. 32.

PEOPLE RIFLE THROUGH YOUR STUFF MAKING CONECTIONS YOU WOULD NOT HAVE DREAMT OFF

body of cultural knowledge, meditate on it, and pass it on intact (possibly a little enlarged) to the children of the elite.'[3]

Alloway had been a key player and spokesperson for the Independent Group (IG), whose interests and activities laid the groundwork for Pop Art in Britain. The IG included artists, architects and historians such as Richard Hamilton, Eduardo Paolozzi, John McHale, Nigel Henderson, Reyner Banham and Alison and Peter Smithson, who met regularly at the ICA between 1952 and 1955 to discuss high modernist art, science, and new technologies on an equal footing to the popular culture of Hollywood Westerns, pulp science fiction, car styling, comic books, advertising and celebrity. This non-hierarchical, or democratised view of high and low art was referred to as 'a fine art-Pop Art continuum'.[4] Alloway's 'Long Front' offered a mass audience with an abundance of variety and choice that challenged both perceived provincialism and cultural elitism – an aesthetics of plenty.

Collage had been a technique developed by the Surrealists to explore the unconscious mind. But for Pop artists, collage was an instrument used to experiment on art itself, to question what it might mean, what its subject could be, to test and explode its boundaries. Richard Hamilton's collage *Just what is it that makes today's homes so different, so appealing?*, was created as an exhibition poster for the Whitechapel Art Gallery's 'This is Tomorrow' exhibition in 1956. The *mise en scène* of a modern, open-

3 Lawrence Alloway, 'The Long Front of Culture', *Cambridge Opinion*, Cambridge University Press, Cambridge, 1959, pp. 25–26.
4 Ibid.

plan sitting room – complete with tootsie pop touting body builder, glamour model and tinned ham – was cut and pasted from a number of American magazines, and is widely acclaimed to be the first, and perhaps most iconic example of British Pop.

Nearly seventy years later – and particularly in light of the global acceleration of (often free) mass communication via the Internet – there are rich seams still to be mined in Alloway's formulation of 'The Long Front of Culture'. Specifically, his theory provides a useful lens through which to view a selection of objects from collections across the Midlands that make up the third of four exhibitions initiated by the Contemporary Art Society and the Whitechapel Gallery.

There are two key, seemingly disparate, focuses of the display that highlight particularly strong aspects of the Midlands' collections. Firstly ceramics, reflecting a local production and industry that dates back to medieval times and was at its zenith during the eighteenth and nineteenth centuries, especially in and around Staffordshire. The other focus of the display is Pop art, which particularly reflects the ambitious acquisition strategies in Wolverhampton and Warwick. These two main areas are supplemented by additional contemporary and historical pieces, and also works of antiquity, to create a kind of free-associative connectiveness that expands on the central theme of value.

This extemporising approach to selecting and assembling the work for the exhibition takes its cue from collage: pots and Pop, images and objects are clustered together in a number of loose, thematic, non-hierarchical groups across which ideas spark, igniting different ways of thinking about meaning and value. Contemporary artist Bob and Roberta Smith engages with the associative freedom that collage permits, and in response to working with material from the Jacob Epstein archive (as discussed below) he makes the bold and celebratory comment, 'People rifle through your stuff and make connections you would not have dreamt off' (sic). It is in this spirit that a range of themes have been picked out here for further elaboration: representations of the human form; the impact of trade and industry on the import and export of style and taste; human rights and protest; and the role that the individual, unique object plays in the age of mass production. A backdrop to this, and a distinctive feature that recurs as a kind of leitmotif for ways of thinking about value, is the role that philanthropy has had in the creation of the museum art collections in the Midlands.

One of the gems of The Herbert Museum and Art Gallery in Coventry is a medieval face jug that was made around 800 years ago, and was excavated in the 1930s near the remains of a priory outside Nuneaton. The anthropomorphisation of vessels was not uncommon at the time, and continues today in the form of the toby jug and other everyday ceramic items. The depiction of the human form is one of the most fundamental instincts for representation and can be seen in the earliest known art of the Ice Age. In the case of the face jug, without knowing the maker's exact meaning or motivation, it evidently must have had something to do with sharing and celebrating the liquid that it held.

A Peruvian vessel in the form of a man's head that dates from 400 to 600 AD, and a small bronze-age Mesopotamian figure, which dates from 3,000 to 2,500 BC are both items in the Garman Ryan Collection at the New Art Gallery Walsall. It contains over 350 works, including those by European artists such as Van Gogh, Monet, Modigliani, Picasso, and Freud, as well as sculpture, vessels and votive objects from Africa, Asia and South American cultures. It also contains the largest public collection of work by Jacob Epstein, which was assembled during the 1960s and early 1970s by his widow Kathleen Garman (following the artist's death in 1959) and her life-long friend Sally Ryan; it was

gifted to the people of Walsall in 1973 and found its permanent home at The New Art Gallery when it was opened in 2000. The Peruvian vessel is an artefact from a burial site, whose function would have been to provide sustenance for the deceased in the afterlife. The votive or totemic importance held by the Peruvian head can also be recognised in the original qualitative value of the Mesopotamian clay figure. It may well be one of many pieces of non-European sculpture that Epstein filled his house and studio with. But although questions about the figure's authenticity have been raised, whether or not it is a fake, its significance for Epstein would have been close to the potency of its original purpose, and how this fed and informed his own concerns as an artist, above all else.

Lord and Lady Attenborough have entrusted their extraordinary collection of Picasso ceramics to the New Walk Museum & Art Gallery in Leicester – the largest private collection of his ceramics in the UK. Many pieces in their collection are unique, but others are in larger editions of up to 500, which were decorated by the highly skilled craftsmen who were able to reproduce the distinctive Picasso style. Throughout his career, Picasso demonstrated that he clearly understood the complex relationship between art, the everyday and the marketplace. Perhaps at times to the exasperation of his dealers, he took immense pleasure in challenging the notion of art's exclusivity and value by prolifically producing both editioned prints and ceramic works in large series or multiples. 'I would have liked to take all these pots, load them on a donkey and drive them to market to sell them for 100 francs each… But then the dealers would find out, and they would buy them and resell them, and it would all have been for nothing.'[5] Picasso's desire to make his work plentiful and affordable for ordinary people was in large part due to his political beliefs. He had joined the Communist party after the war and was active in the peace movement, which adopted his drawing of a dove as their instantly recognisable symbol at the inaugural Peace Congress in Paris in 1949.

5 *Picasso Ceramics: The Attenborough Collection*, Marilyn McCully & Michael Raeburn (eds.), New Walk Museum & Art Gallery, Leicester, 2007, p. 21

Pots have always played much more than a purely functional role within domestic environments. They provide clues and indications of an owner's status, how they lived and what they believed in and can reveal social and economic structures. China was the first country in the world to produce porcelain over 800 years ago, and one of the most explicit examples of cultural migration can be recognised in the trade and enduring influence of Chinese ceramics. The striking contrast of cobalt blue against white is a method of decoration that is now instantly associated with Chinese porcelain, but it was originally adopted from their trade during the early Middle Ages with what is now Iran and Iraq. By the sixteenth century there were highly developed trade routes between China and Europe and by the mid-eighteenth century thousands of tons of blue and white Chinese porcelain were shipped to London each year. A large variety of patterns and decorations were specifically developed for the European export market, often rendering European scenes or symbols in distinctive Chinese style and context. The high levels of output of handmade ceramics in England, Europe and China meant the cross-fertilisation of style, taste and fashion through global trade, but the purchase of imported goods remained the preserve of the wealthy. Staffordshire had been a centre for ceramic production since the early seventeenth century, but industrialisation saw the mass production of ceramics grow to its height from 1800 to 1860. Serial methods of production and decoration enabled the potteries to standardise their wares and keep costs significantly lower, so that more and more people were able to buy British versions of a Chinese idea of British taste for an exoticised East.

The introduction of transfer printing onto ceramics was developed in the mid-1700s. The blue and white willow pattern is perhaps one of the most recognisable transfer printed decorations to be found on English tableware. Despite its appearance, it is a pseudo-Chinese vignette taken from a variety of sources that was designed by the potter Thomas Minton in Stoke around 1790, and is still used today. So ubiquitous

was this scene in homes across England and America, it became a kind of shorthand for middle-class erudition and good taste. It is no coincidence that American sculptor Jann Haworth chose the design for her soft sculpture cups and saucers that form part of her iconic pop work *Donuts, Coffee Cups and Comics* (1962), from Wolverhampton Art Gallery's collection.

A consequence of the increased affordable availability of transfer-printed decorated pots and tableware for everyday use in the home, was the increase in volume of ceramics whose purpose was to commemorate or celebrate events, individuals or groups. The mass reproducibility of the technology meant that ceramics were the ideal vehicle for expounding the achievements of Victorian design, manufacture and trade. A densely decorated octagonal platter made in Queen Victoria's jubilee year of 1887 announces the precise import and export figures for 1885, in addition to providing the total population and total land area in square miles, not just of Great Britain, but of the entire British Empire, on which we are also reminded 'the sun never sets'. At a more local level, a domestic transfer-printed jug has been appropriated and refashioned with scratched images of workers at traditional hand looms to bid 'Success to the Jolly Ribbon Weavers' of Coventry – communicating personal and community pride in and through artisanal skills at a time when the machine was threatening livelihoods. This rousing and hearty ethos is also seen on a small child's mug colourfully decorated with bees swarming around a hive and proclaiming 'Industry – Learn to Live'.

Ceramic manufacture in England has played a significant role in the expression of political beliefs and affiliations as a result of a sense of growing political freedoms since the seventeenth century. Social commentary through caricature and satire has a strong tradition in England, with William Hogarth being the most prominent in the eighteenth century. Artists such as James Gillray, Isaac Cruikshank and his son George continued this tradition in the nineteenth century through prints, book illustration and broadsheets, which were at times also adapted for transfer printing onto mass-produced ceramics. Support for specific people and causes as well as proclamations against individuals, including the monarchy, frequently found their way onto pots for use in the home. A portrait of Queen Caroline, the rejected and tragic wife of the philandering and unpopular George IV, who became King in 1820, appears on jugs that declare the public's outrage for 'Caroline, our much injured Queen'. Printed on a small, inexpensively produced teapot is Kipling's patriotic poem 'The Absent Minded Beggar', which was first published by the *Daily Mail* in 1899 as part of their appeal to raise funds for the soldiers who were fighting in the South African War. This and other related merchandise raised around £250,000 (about £20 million today), and is a clear example of the sorts of messages that could be communicated by an everyday ceramic item beyond its regular function. Such pots acted directly within wider society, as well as in the home.

Paul Scott's work today also employs the traditions and techniques of transfer-printed ware by making interventions with recycled, often damaged or imperfect, cheaply purchased and salvaged ceramics. For Scott, the industrial history of mass-produced ceramics and what can be interpreted from the designs and patterns that they bear, offer a rich platform for contemporary social comment. He regularly engages with the decorative conceit found in the English taste for Chinoiserie and representations of imaginary idylls to make stringent observations 'about our complacency over the loss of industrial skills and the economic and social consequences for those people who were engaged in production'.[6] Incorporated into familiar blue and white scenes of the English countryside, one is wrong-footed when a fighter plane is spotted streaking across the rural skies, or wind turbines tower behind country cottages. After the closure of the Spode factory in Stoke-on-Trent in 2009, Scott was given permission to collect abandoned items from the defunct site. In the spirit of Marcel Duchamp's assisted readymades, he worked both with decorated tableware and with some plain bone chine plates, which 'were cleaned up and used as the vehicle for a series of in-glaze screenprints depicting the factory in its death throes'.[7]

Childs's mug 'Industry – Learn to Live', c.1840, lusterware with beehive motif, 6 x 6.5 cm. Courtesy Nottingham City Museums and Galleries

Jug in support of 'Caroline our much injured Queen', c.1820, Staffordshire earthenware, transfer-printed and hand-decorated, 10 x 13.5 x 9.5 cm. Courtesy of The Potteries Museum & Art Gallery, Stoke-on-Trent

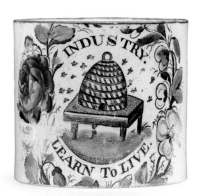

6 Correspondence with Paul Scott, January 2013.
7 Ibid.

Another searingly poignant iteration in the tradition of English commemorative ceramics is Scott's *Cockle Pickers* tea service that was produced in 2007 to mark the bicentenary of the passing of the parliamentary bill to abolish the slave trade in Britain. For Scott, 'The quintessentially English "cup of tea" and tea service are inextricably linked with Britain's development of the slave trade.'[8] The work refers specifically to the tragedy when, in 2004, 23 Chinese cockle pickers, employed illegally on starvation wages, were cut off and drowned by an incoming tide in Morecambe Bay: 'In spite of its formal legal abolition, slavery is still with us in the twenty-first century manifesting itself in a number of ways, but almost always involving illegal immigrants forced to work or live in appalling conditions by gang masters.'[9]

Scott's tackling of universal issues such as human rights and slavery has very specific precedents in a small ceramic medallion produced by Josiah Wedgwood in his state of the art pottery factory in 1787. 'AM I NOT A MAN AND A BROTHER?' is a statement that appears on a cameo relief of a kneeling black male with clasped hands bound in chains. Presented against a light-coloured background, the half-clad figure was the most famous image of a black person in eighteenth century art, instantly identifying its wearer with the slavery abolitionist movement. Thousands of these medallions were produced and distributed primarily for free, and quickly became a public declaration of one's affiliations that was powerfully recognisable. Wedgwood sent these medallions to Benjamin Franklin, one of the Founding Fathers of the United States, and they were an immediate success. The anti-slavery campaigner Thomas Clarkson commented at the time:

8 Ibid.
9 Ibid.

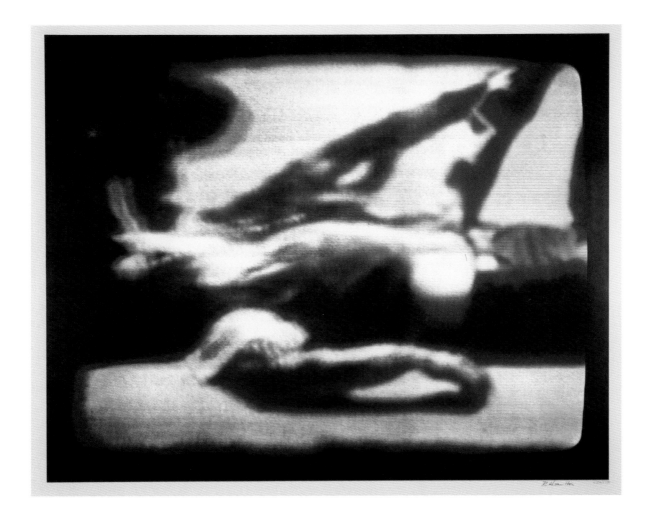

'ladies wore them in bracelets, and others had them fitted up in an ornamental manner as pins for their hair. At length the taste for wearing them became general, and thus fashion, which usually confines itself to worthless things, was seen for once in the honorable office of promoting the cause of justice, humanity and freedom.'[10]

Many Pop artists also had a fundamental understanding of the power of conflating the political with the popular, and how to utilise the technologies of the day to exploit the potential for getting messages into the public consciousness. A key element of Richard Hamilton's practice is printmaking, and this is an area that he and a number of Pop artists were engaged with throughout their careers. Not only did he seek to stretch the technical possibilities of the medium, he also saw the potential for prints to be a powerful way of distributing his work to large audiences.[11] For Hamilton and others, however, popular culture was not confined to consumerism, celebrity and advertising, it was also at times highly politicised. In 1970 Hamilton produced a screenprint, *Kent State* in an edition of 5,000 to 'ensure that the print could be sold cheaply and the price would not rise unduly afterwards'.[12] The image was based on a photograph he had snapped from a television broadcast about the Ohio National Guard's shooting of four students

10 Thomas Clarkson, *The History of the Rise, Progress and Abolition of the African Slave Trade by the British Parliament*, John S. Taylor, New York, 1836, Vol. 3, p.297.
11 This idea perhaps found its most complete expression in his design for The Beatles' *White Album* poster, which was inserted into each record sleeve as an unlimited – though numbered – edition of many millions.
12 Richard Hamilton, *Collected Words 1953-1982*, Thames and Hudson Ltd., London, 1982, p. 95.

Midlands

protesting against America's involvement in the Vietnam War. The blurred image of one of the students lying shot on the ground is both a form of contemporary history painting – coming from a European tradition that references Goya and Manet – as well as an investigation of the way in which the exploding consumer culture via television is able to erase deeply felt divisions between high art and contemporary subject matter. Hamilton was initially reluctant to use this image because 'it was too terrible an incident in American history to submit to arty treatment. Yet... It seemed right, too, that art could help to keep the shame in our minds: the wide distribution of a large edition print might be the strongest indictment I could make.'[13]

Hamilton was later to subject not just one, but a number of terrible events to 'arty treatment' in a 1992 remake of his 1965 *Just what is it...* collage. Like *Kent State*, it was produced in an edition of 5,000 – on this occasion as the subject of a BBC television programme in the series *QED* called 'Art and Chips', which invited the artist to employ computer technology as a tool to make art. Using a Quantel Paintbox, his updated version was a computer-generated 'collage' that included images of the Gulf War, starvation in Ethiopia, Fluck and Law's caricature of Margaret Thatcher, AIDS, the economic market and other aspects of contemporary society and globalism. They were printed on an A4 colour printer, signed and numbered by Hamilton, and distributed free to 5,000 viewers who had written in to the programme. A unique marriage of new technology meets mass media, meets contemporary culture and politics. Just as the television programme entered into people's homes, so did the print.

Andy Warhol's *Birmingham Race Riot* (1964) also engages with contemporary politics and the media, confronting issues that resonate with Wedgwood's abolitionist medallion produced 200 years earlier. It is a screenprint taken from a newspaper

13 Ibid.

photograph of the violent response by the white authorities to one of the non-violent civil rights protests of black youth in Alabama in spring 1963. These confrontations are acknowledged as having triggered the March on Washington for Jobs and Freedom in August that year, at which Martin Luther King Jr. delivered his now legendary 'I have a dream' speech. This was the largest peaceful demonstration for human rights ever held in the US and is credited with influencing the passing of the Civil Rights and the Voting Rights Acts in the subsequent two years. The timing of the production of this print is key, because while capturing a moment of extreme civil unrest, its publication took place when real progress towards civil rights seemed to be made. Warhol was not an overtly political animal, but acutely understood the immense power of mass media and how it could both affect and reflect the popular mood of the people. This print was one in a portfolio of ten that contained America's most prominent contemporary artists. It was produced in an edition of 500 by Sam Wagstaff, the curator of the Wadsworth Atheneum in Hartford, Connecticut, whose ambition with these prints was to offer people 'as big a hunk of the current aesthetic as they could as cheaply as possible'.[14]

Peter Blake was also keen to tap into the current aesthetic in this way as is demonstrated by *Babe Rainbow,* a screenprint onto tin of a fictitious woman wrestler that was produced in an edition of 10,000 in 1967. As well as being fascinated with American popular culture, his brand of Pop also reflected a specifically post-war British aesthetic that drew on the vernacular of the fairground or the end-of-the-pier show. This mood is perfectly captured in Ken Russell's 1962 film portrait of Blake, along with artists Pauline Boty, Derek Boshier and Peter Phillips, *Pop Goes the Easel.* His friend, the guitarist and songwriter of The Who, Pete Townshend stated that *Babe Rainbow* was his favourite piece:

Patrick
Caulfield,
Pink Jug, 1981,
screenprint,
edition of 80,
98.5 x 80 cm.
Courtesy of
University of
Warwick Art
Collection ©
The Estate
of Patrick
Caulfield.
All rights
reserved,
DACS 2014

OPPOSITE
Peter Blake,
Babe Rainbow,
1967,
screenprint
on tin, edition
of 10, 000,
66 x 44.1 cm.
Courtesy of
University
of Warwick
Art Collection
© Peter Blake.
All rights
reserved,
DACS 2014

14 Sam Wagstaff as quoted in University of Warwick information sheet.

Jug, Undated, Winchcombe Pottery, Gloucestershire stoneware, 20.5 x 15 x 18.5 cm. Courtesy of University of Warwick Art Collection

OPPOSITE Posset pot, maker's initials IB and RF, 1696, Staffordshire earthenware, decorated in coloured slips, 15 x 28 x 22 cm. Courtesy of The Potteries Museum & Art Gallery, Stoke-on-Trent

'It sold in Carnaby Street, a totally appropriate place, for about £1. I love the fact that it was mass produced and freely available and yet still a work to be treasured (like a record). The innocent ikonisation of real and imagined heroes of the boxing and circus rings reminding me very much of an aspect of pop-music and its audiences' fickle adulation of the colourful characters who pass through their trash tabloids and over their record player decks.'[15]

The flip side to mass production is of course the unique, individual work of art. Between these two poles sit those objects that are neither machine-produced, nor elevated to fine art, and this is applied art or craft. Twentieth century studio pottery occupies an important position in relation to both high art and the machine made, emerging as a result of the revival of craftsmanship that had been expounded by a number of late-nineteenth century thinkers and artists such as William Morris and those involved in the Arts and Crafts movement, who rejected what they saw to be the de-humanising effects of industrialisation. However socialist Morris was in his advocacy of economic and social reform, the works of fine and decorative art that were the products of the Arts and Crafts movement remained unavailable to the vast proportion of poor and working-class people in Britain. Bernard Leach was keenly aware of and much admired the Arts and Crafts ethos, but having spent the first few years of his life in both Hong Kong and Japan before returning there as a student in his twenties, his approach to craftsmanship was less associated with political beliefs and had more to do with his engagement with eastern philosophy. The writer on ceramics Oliver Watson describes Leach's huge influence on twentieth century studio pottery and the trend for plain, utilitarian ceramics as the 'ethical pot', which is 'lovingly made in the correct way and with the correct attitude, [and] would contain a spiritual and moral dimension.'[16]

15 Pete Townshend, p.4 of the booklet produced alongside Peter Blake's 1984 Tate catalogue.
16 Oliver Watson, *Studio Pottery*, Phaidon Press Limited, London, 1990, p. 15.

Two potters who worked under Leach in the 1920s were Michael Cardew and Katherine Pleydell-Bouverie. Cardew's early work looked to the pre-industrial English tradition of slipware ceramics and defiantly rejected factory production. Despite recognition, his struggle to make a living for himself and his family meant he became increasingly aware of the inherent contradictions that underlined the desire for an authentic, 'ethical pot' for everyday use, and how this could ever be economically viable for the average wage earner in a post-industrial, capitalist society. Financial and intrinsic values were forever at loggerheads for Cardew. Pleydell-Bouverie's aesthetic ideals chimed with Cardew's, but being from a wealthy aristocratic background she had no need to make a living from her work, and so was able to produce exactly what she wanted – primarily small bowls and vases – and could happily sell the work at a relatively low price. The simplicity of her unadorned vessels embodies orientalist traditions communicated by Leach, but equally they signal her ambition for an introspective modernist aesthetic.

Two unique pots form part of the collection at The Potteries Museum and Art Gallery in Stoke-on-Trent. The older of the two is part of the outstanding collection of local Staffordshire ceramics accessioned into the ceramics collection, whereas the more contemporary is a work by Grayson Perry that has been accessioned as fine art. The earlier piece is a slipware posset pot dated 1696 that bears the inscription 'THE BEST IS NOT TOO GOOD FOR YOU'.[17] It also bears the initials IB and RF, which are either those of the maker or those of the person for whom the pot was made – or both. This is one of a few dozen pots of this design that are known, which tell us that this particular style, decoration and motto was fashionable for around thirty years. Though over 300 years ago, when the average household would have had a minimum of material belongings, the message has a contemporary ring to it and sounds as if it could have been conceived as an advertising strapline for luxury goods – 'because you're worth it'. Decorated in slip with tulip designs and geometric patterns, they would have been prized possessions and put on display in the homes of comfortable, but by no means the wealthiest, families at that time and used for celebrations and commemorations.

Perry's pot is a large hand-built vase entitled *Designer Rebellion*, made in 1999. It too is an object to be placed on show and admired, but unlike the posset pot, it has no practical or ceremonial function and its destiny would have been the home

17 Posset was a nourishing and sometimes medicinal drink of curdled milk, eggs, sugar, alcohol and spices.

Grayson Perry,
*Designer
Rebellion*,
1999, glazed
ceramic, 85.8
x 33 x 33 cm.
The Potteries
Museum & Art
Gallery, Stoke-
on-Trent;
purchased
through the
Contemporary
Art Society
Special
Collection
Scheme
with Lottery
funding from
Arts Council
England, 2000.
Courtesy the
artist and
Victoria Miro,
London ©
Grayson Perry

of a well-heeled collector, or, in this case, The Potteries Museum as a purchase through the Contemporary Art Society. And like the posset pot, it also includes text. It is covered in horizontally stamped words that repeat on alternate lines: *destroy destroy destroy.* Between each of these lines are the names of various personalities in contemporary art and culture – *Hirst Hirst Hirst* – *Starck Starck Starck* – *Saatchi Saatchi Saatchi* – *Serota Serota Serota* and so forth. Integrated among the text is incised and transfer-printed imagery of skateboarders and youth culture. The density of the surface pattern and the classic form of the vase obscures an immediate interpretation of the pot's message, and is only revealed on closer scrutiny. Like Paul Scott's manipulation of blue and white tradition, this wrong-footing of one's preconceptions is a ploy that Perry often uses: 'I like the whole iconography of pottery. It hasn't got any pretentions to being great public works of art, and no matter how brash a statement I make, on a pot it will always have a certain humility.'[18]

For last year's Reith Lectures, Perry made four presentations called 'Playing to the Gallery'. Whether or not he would today choose to rile against *all* of the individuals that he picked out for destruction on *Designer Rebellion* is perhaps debatable, but throughout his career he has continued to acknowledge the complex and at times contradictory relationship between what contemporary artists do, and how their work becomes consumed by the art world and the general public. He consistently questions what defines good and bad taste and is acutely aware of the interconnectedness between the various ranks of validation (the commercial gallery, the critic, the collector, the media, the auction house, and ultimately the museum curator) that all need to be in agreement before a consensus of what is the best art can be reached.

Like Lawrence Alloway's 'keepers of the flame', Perry's 'validation chorus' ultimately also bestows value. But there has been a shift in the intervening seventy or so years between these two declarations. Bringing his post-Marxist ideology to the subject, Alloway's analysis saw the elite as primarily defined by the privileged classes whose status was determined as much by their education and intellect as by their income. Perry's definition, however, is not one that is determined by a political or ideological position, or a centuries-old notion of class, but more directly by purchase power. But neither position can ever provide us with the final word on how we assess the best. To define value in relation to art – as much as to the material stuff of our daily lives – is an attempt to understand that which is continually in flux and is subtly recalibrating according to a range of factors such as time, place, fashion and availability. However, these extrinsic factors can also coexist with personal or symbolic qualities, which have less to do with materiality and more to do with a kind of universality of meaning. This intrinsic kind of value is by definition tricky to articulate, but – even without the 'validation chorus' or the 'keepers of the flame' to defend it – it can also be more enriching.

My aim was not to throw a spotlight onto some of the well-known or treasured works from collections in the Midlands as a way of broadening our understanding of the region's artistic, social and cultural history. Instead, I have sought out some of the more commonplace objects and items that have now found their way into these collections, but were originally meant to be lived with. Returning to the posset pot, although it now takes pride of place in The Potteries Museum & Art Gallery's collection, its motto provides a fundamental indication of its original value and purpose. Its worth can be measured financially, but the message, as intended by its maker, THE BEST IS NOT TOO GOOD FOR YOU, proposes something altogether more generous, which is about giving *you* – everyone – the best.

18 Grayson Perry, *Guerrilla Tactics*, Stedelijk Museum, Amsterdam, 2002, p.38.

Ingrid Swenson

Animating Photography: Double Exposure and the Magic of Movement

Gaia Tedone

When Collecting Makes History

There is something utterly magical about studying a private collection, as the process unveils the intricate interweaving of a person's life trajectory and a specific historical narrative. If the collector is a respected historian and has an identical twin brother, then the overlaps are even greater, and the formation of the collection and the events of a lifetime are ultimately inextricable. This is the case with the early cinema collection that inspired the fourth display in the series drawn from the Contemporary Art Society's membership of museums. In responding to the theme 'the role of individuals in creating visions for particular collections' in relation to the South of England, my attention was immediately drawn to the collection assembled by film historian John Barnes (1920–2008) and his twin brother William (b.1920).

John and William began collecting at the age of 13. Their collection traces the evolution of the moving image from the period film historians refer to as 'the archaeology of cinema', until the pioneering work of the British filmmakers from the south coast identified with the 'The Brighton School'.[1] A joint effort, which combined scientific rigour with great passion, William was 'the archaeologist' who explored the hidden corners of flea markets to find the best bargains or rarities to resell in his Chelsea market stall. John was 'the interpreter', supporting his brother's discoveries by fact-checking, researching provenance, and corresponding with whoever was in possession of any useful fragments of information.

The Barnes brothers' fascination with cinema began in 1931, when a relative gave them an early Phatescope camera and a projector to distract them after the death of their father. Their years of dedicated research and collecting culminated in a detailed five-volume history of British Cinema written by John Barnes, and the opening of the Barnes Brothers Museum of Cinematography in St. Ives.[2] The museum, which they ran from 1963 for more than twenty years, attracted half a million visitors. A large blow-up of an Eadweard Muybridge sequence was one of the first images the visitor would see, possibly making quite an impact on Francis Bacon during his recurring visits.[3] The Barnes collection comprises the distinct vision of two informed individuals, yet it is also an account of the history of collecting a specific medium, film, which at the time was relatively undocumented.

Inspiring the Barnes brothers' initial journey into cinema history was the film collection of Wilfred Ernest Lytton Day (1873–1936), one of the best-known figures in the history of early British Cinema. The Will Day Collection was, at the time, displayed at the Science Museum in London, before moving to the Cinémathèque Française in Paris. Sadly, the integrity of the collection the Barnes brothers put together did not survive. The closing of their museum in St. Ives marked the decisive split of the two most important parts of the collection: the National Cinema Museum in Turin acquired the material related to the archaeology of cinema – shadowgraphs, panoramas, Dioramas, magic lanterns and optical toys – while Hove Museum absorbed all the material relating to the south coast film-makers, thanks to the key role played by Dr. Frank Gray, Curator of the Screen Archive South East.

'Twixt Two Worlds' attempts, albeit partially, to reconnect the two parts of the Barnes Collection through a few key loans from the museum in Turin. The curatorial framework of this display emerges out of the excavation of the material stored at Hove and is inspired by the Barnes brothers' work as researchers, their exhaustive approach as collectors and their unique relationship as identical twins.

A key accomplishment of their collection is the distinct articulation of the transition

1 Laurent Mannoni proposed the term 'archaeology of the cinema' in 1995, in order to describe a kind of prehistory of the medium, pointing to the techniques of projections and photographic technologies that recreated the illusion of movement and preceded the advent of film.
2 Vol.1: *The Beginnings of Cinema in England*, David & Charles, London, 1976; Vol.2: *The Rise of the Cinema in Great Britain*, Bishopsgate, London, 1983; Vol.3: *Pioneers of the British Film*, Bishopsgate, London, 1988; Vol.4: *Filming the Boer War*, Bishopsgate, London, 1992; Vol.5: *The Beginnings of the Cinema in England, 1894–1901,* University of Exeter Press, Exeter, 1997.
3 During an interview, yet to be published, William Barnes mentions how Francis Bacon was a frequent visitor of the museum. Such visits probably enhanced the artist's fascination with the work of Eadweard Muybridge, which greatly influenced his treatment of the human body.

Eadweard
Muybridge,
Animal
Locomotion
Series.
Courtesy Royal
Pavilion and
Museums,
Brighton
& Hove

between the still and the moving image, across a variety of optical and projection devices. It documents the historical circumstances and fervid disputes that surrounded their invention, commercialisation and social use. 'Twixt Two Worlds' developed organically out of this fertile ground and looks at the technique of double exposure and the visual effect of superimposition as starting points to explore the animation of the image across photography, the magic lantern and cinema. While looking at this transition in both historical and technical terms, it also attempts to articulate a parallel trajectory, which considers the use of doubling as a suggestive vehicle to signal the apparition of 'another world' – a world ruled by the laws of imagination, illusion and paranormal phenomena. In the space between these two worlds, only separated by the cinematic screen, the tensions between science and magic, vision and insanity, life and death crucially play out.

This essay wishes to explore a number of these tensions, while providing a broader contextualisation of some of the works, historical and contemporary, included in the display. It will begin by focusing on different iterations of the technique of double exposure across spirit photography, dissolving views slides and 'trick films'. It will then trace a trajectory of the moving image, through the development of instantaneous photography and chronophotography, the term coined by French physiologist Étienne-Jules Marey (1830–1904) to define a set of photographs of a moving object, and their relationship with capturing time. While the first layer leads towards the world of the fantastic, through the moving image's associations with natural magic, the second highlights the affiliation with scientific and technological innovation. The recurring references to a number of key practices (hypnosis and telepathy) and iconographic symbols (the skeleton and the hysterical woman) cut across both science and magic, capturing their intimate connection in Victorian popular culture.

Fluid Traces and Circular Visions

In 'A short history of superimposition: From spirit photography to early cinema' (2012), Simone Natale traces an account of superimposition effects in photography, stage magic, magic lanterns, and cinema, highlighting how the 'visual representation of ghosts in the nineteenth century wavered between religion and spectacle, fiction and realism, and still and moving pictures.'[4] The role of spiritualism during the Victorian era has been described as 'a pervasive and potent force at all levels of society and culture' and as 'a key participant in the cultural expression of animation and visibility that generated much pictorial, literary and theatrical production.'[5] Spirit photography emerged out of this particular context and became a widespread practice in the 1860s. Much like the other activities through which the spiritualist movement operated, it attracted the attention of those who were willing to believe in it, and those who wished to expose it. The Mediums and the magicians operated at the two opposite ends of this spectrum, with the latter preferring to align themselves with science, through honest illusion, rather than the spiritual trickery and supernatural forces associated with spiritualism.[6] Thanks to the technique of multiple exposure and superimposition, the photographic medium found itself in the midst of such animated dispute. The proposition that photography could detect and register what the human eye was unable to see, providing a direct access to spirits and ghosts, was no doubt attractive, satisfying the pervasive obsession with the 'other side'.

It is around the case of the Medium William Eglinton (1857–1933) that believers and non-believers of the spiritualist movement found a concrete battle to fight. 'Twixt Two Worlds' references the book written by John Farmer in 1886 that presents an account of the life and professional career of Eglinton, from his sceptical beginnings

4 Simone Natale, 'A short history of superimposition: From spirit photography to early cinema', *Early Popular Visual Culture*, Vol.10, No.2, 2012, pp.125–45.
5 Lynda Nead, *The Haunted Gallery: Painting, Photography, Film c.1900*, Yale University Press, New Haven, 2007.
6 Ibid.

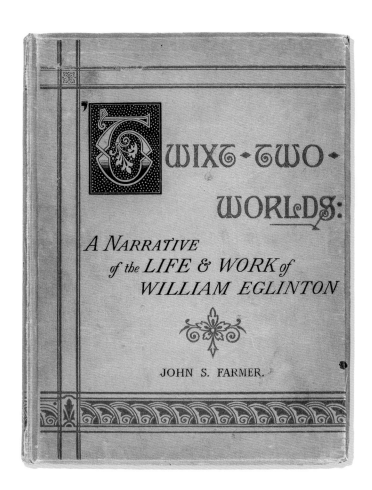

John Stephen Farmer, *Twixt Two Worlds: A Narrative of the Life and Work of William Eglinton*, 1886, book cover with frontispiece illustration by James Tissot. Published by Psychological Press, London. The Mitchell Wolfson, Jr. Collection. Published with the permission of The Wolfsonian – Florida International University (Miami, Florida). Photo: David Almeida

in London in 1874 to his seance with the Russian Emperor Alexander III in 1887.[7] A rare group of spirit photographs has survived from the last phase of Eglinton's career, and today belongs to the Brighton and Hove Museums collections. The prints were discovered a few years ago, during an inventory of the photographic collection, presenting an unprecedented and valuable addition to the museum's holdings. At the time of the discovery, they immediately attracted the curiosity and attention of Kevin Bacon, then Curator of Photographs. The outcome of his study and research culminated in the article 'The Medium's Medium' published in 2008 in *The Royal Pavilion Review*.[8]

Five prints in particular stand out in the group, but interestingly, Eglinton does not appear in any of them. Mounted in cabinet format, they were produced between 1886 and 1887 by Mary Burchett, the woman who can be seen in most of them. Each print bears a handwritten note on the reverse of the mount, describing the particular circumstances under which each image was produced, or the name of the spirit – Joey Sandy and Ernest for instance – that Eglinton used to invoke during his seances. The relationship between Eglinton and Burchett remains unclear; it is up to the viewer to decide whether she was a genuine believer or accomplice in the Medium's exploitation of photographic tricks. As Bacon seems to suggest, the note written on the reverse of the photograph taken and developed on 27 October 1886 supports the first option. The print shows Burchett's face obscured by a shrouded arm and the note reads as follows: 'I took my own photograph with the aid of the automatic tube, of course the spirit hand which appears in front of me was not visible to me'. Burchett is also referenced in Farmer's book, in which she is described carrying a photograph of her Austrian spirit friend 'V' in her pocket. Such a detail, alongside the small format of the prints, offers a precious insight into the social function of spirit photographs; they were physically carried around as 'records

7 Twixt is an abbreviation for betwixt, an archaic form of the word between.
8 Kevin Bacon contextualises the prints within the broader historical practice of spirit photography and frames them as evidence of Eglinton's declining professional career, a last and rather unconvincing attempt to regain popularity after he became abruptly overshadowed. These were not the only spirit photographs Eglinton produced during his career as a medium. Alexander Aksakov, advisor to the Tsar and a fervent supporter of spiritualism, took another series during Eglinton's trip to Russia, which marked the end of his career as a psychic guide.

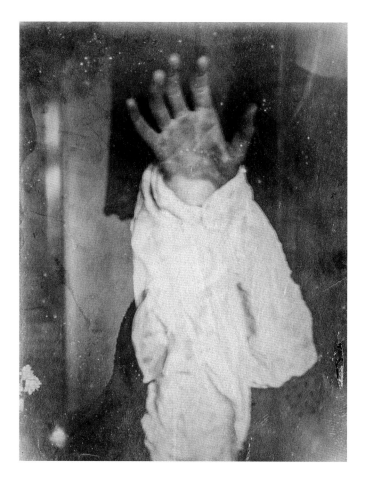

of personal pain and grief' rather than 'relics of a strange and fraudulent practice'.[9]

The vague circumstances under which these photographs ended up within the Royal Pavilion and Museums, Brighton & Hove collections reinforces the mysterious narrative around them. According to the curator's accounts, an anonymous collector donated them in the late 1970s. I happily position myself among a small group of advocates who would like to believe that they originally belonged to the private collection of Hove-based film pioneer George Albert Smith (1864–1959). Although not a shred of evidence has been found in support of this theory, their lives and careers did overlap. George Albert Smith was a hypnotist, mesmerist and magic lanternist, who shared with Eglinton a vivid engagement with the 'other side', which resulted in the production of the 'first manifestation of the ghost illusion in British film'. [10]

Eglinton and Smith knew each other: Smith attended eight of Eglinton's 'Slate-Writing' seances when he was working for the Society of Psychical Research (SPR) – an organisation founded in 1882, with the mission to conduct scholarly research into human experiences that challenged scientific models. Having established his reputation performing experiments with Thought Reading at the Brighton Aquarium, with his colleague Douglas Blackburn, Smith joined the society from 1883 until 1887 in the capacity of personal assistant for the Honorary Secretary Mr. Edmund Gurney. Among the different activities that Smith undertook for the SPR, he co-authored the paper 'Experiments in Thought-Transference' for the Society's journal (1889), and contributed to the ongoing investigation of the presupposed fraudulent activity of Eglinton with a number of reports. As Tom Ruffles eloquently summarised, these reports, although generally in favour of the medium, contributed to the fervent debate among those who believed that Eglinton had psychic abilities, and the more sceptical wing, resulting in a rupture within the structure of the organisation.[11]

9 Kevin Bacon, 'The Medium's Medium', *The Royal Pavilion Review*, February 2008.

10 Frank Gray, 'George Albert Smith's visions and transformations: the films of 1898', in *Visual Delights. Essays on the Popular and Projected Image in the 19th Century* by Simon Popple & Vanessa Toulmin (eds.), Flick Books, Trowbridge, 2000.

11 Tom Ruffles is a former SPR archivist who generously shared his notes drawn together from various references in the Society for Psychical Research's literature.

Did Smith ever come across this group of spirit photographs? And, if he did, how did he react to them? Within the context of the display, the juxtaposition between Eglinton's spirit photographs and Smith's early films wishes to not only draw attention to their distinct use of double exposure and superimposition techniques, but also present them as both products and symptoms of a common cultural background.

The Double Life of the Magic Lantern

The formation of this shared cultural background is closely connected to the life and development of an admirable machine, the magic lantern. Designed by Dutch inventor Christiaan Huygens in the middle of the seventeenth century, this optical projector

Portrait of film pioneer George Albert Smith, copy of black and white photograph taken at his desk with film measurer and Urban Bioscope camera in the Science Museum. The photo was originally taken c.1900. From the Barnes Brothers Collection, Hove Museum. Courtesy Royal Pavilion and Museums, Brighton & Hove

uses a concave mirror at the back of a light source to direct the light through a small rectangular sheet of glass, the lantern slide, onto a lens at the front of the apparatus.[12] As Frank Gray has explained, the magic lantern played a key role in the trajectory of the illuminated image across the centuries and was particularly relevant in establishing the fundamental parameters of screen practice. These consisted of:

> 'the projection onto a screen of a set of related imagery; the organisation of such imagery into a particular narrative order; an audience in a darkened room, seated in rows facing a projection screen; the presence of a lecturer to provide imagery with an oral commentary.'[13]

The term 'magic lantern' suggests the apparatus' early association with both the worlds of science and magic. In the early magic shows, the lantern was usually hidden from the public and its 'covert' use enabled conjurers to perform their tricks, through expedients such as mobile back projections. The Phantasmagoria, invented in Paris around 1794 by Étienne-Gaspard Robert, was the most popular kind of these shows. It involved the creation of an immersive environment, where images were projected,

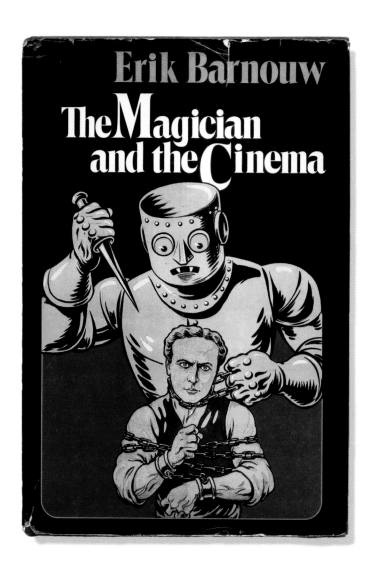

12 As John Barnes pointed out, for quite some time the invention was erroneously attributed to Athanasius Kircher. However, in his famous book *Ars Magna Lucis et Umbrae,* published in 1645–46, there is no account of any apparatus that can be called a magic lantern.

13 Frank Gray, *L'École de Brighton (The Brighton School),* Abbeville Press, New York, 2005, p.21.

THE OPTICAL
MAGIC LANTERN
— JOURNAL —
AND
PHOTOGRAPHIC ENLARGER.

A Magazine of Popular Science for the Lecture-room and the Domestic Circle.

Edited by J. HAY TAYLOR.

[Entered at Stationers' Hall.]

Vol. 5.—No. 67.   DECEMBER 1, 1894.   Xmas No., price 2d., Post-free 3½d.

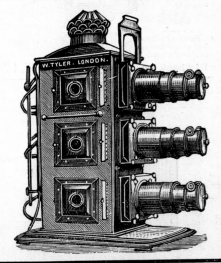

THE PROJECTED IMAGE
A Short History of Magic Lantern Slides

JOHN BARNES

In the second part of the *Catalogue of the Barnes Museum of Cinematography*,[1] we traced the evolution of the magic lantern as an optical instrument, but the history of projection would not be complete without some consideraton of the pictures that were projected. As a writer on the magic lantern observed in 1866,

A magic lantern without a collection of slides may not inappropriately be compared to a theatre without scenery or actors.[2]

Evidence suggests that the invention of the magic lantern, or optical projector, is due to Christiaan Huygens in the middle of the 17th century, and whereas a few facts are known about Huygens' lantern, nothing at all seems to have been recorded about the kind of pictures that were used with it and we can only say that they were transparent paintings on glass.

There was obviously no difficulty involved in improvising coloured slides at this period. Paintings on glass had already existed for a considerable time, even as transparencies to be viewed by transmitted light in the manner of stained glass windows, and narrative scenes had been depicted on all manner of glassware such as drinking glasses and goblets for example. The merest daub painted on a piece of glass was sufficient to display the optical powers of the magic lantern, provided the colours were made sufficiently transparent.

The Jesuit Father, Athanasius Kircher, often, but erroneously regarded as the inventor of the magic lantern, was perhaps the first to direct attention to the kind of slides used with the instrument, and in the second edition of his book, *Ars magna lucis et umbrae*, published in 1671, the engravings depicting two rather fanciful representations of the magic lantern provide a few particulars regarding the slides. In the first engraving (1) a slide is

shown in position in the lantern (although not inverted as, of course, it should be). It is depicted as a long narrow frame of wood, inset with eight glass discs upon which the pictures are painted. On the end of the wooden frame is a small lug or boss, presumably designed for holding when pushing the slide past the objective lens. A similar arrangement is also shown on the frame in the second engraving (2) but here the slide is depicted somewhat foreshortened and it is impossible to determine the number of pictures it is supposed to contain since only two are discernable, but obviously it conforms to the same pattern as the former. The figures which are suggested on both of these slides are too indistinct to be properly identified, but the images of two of the pictures are shown projected on the wall and are of a rather macabre nature. The first seems to resemble a soul in Purgatory engulfed in flames, and the second, the figure of death holding his traditional hour-glass and scythe. Similar 'frightful representations' were henceforth to serve the magic lantern for a long time to come.

A contemporary of Kircher's, Johann Christoph Sturm (1635–1703) who had a better understanding than Kircher, of the optical principles involved and was first to publish an illustration of the instrument in a practical form (3) also provides an interesting example of a magic lantern slide, the subject of which is a head of Bacchus, the Greek god of wine – the first screen closeup?[3] (4)

Johannes Zahn, who gives the most comprehensive coverage of the magic lantern of any writer during the 17th century, describes and illustrates (5) several lanterns using slides of the Kircher type, but he also includes a lantern of a different kind designed for projecting a number of pictures painted upon a glass disc.[4] Circular slides were not generally used however, until the

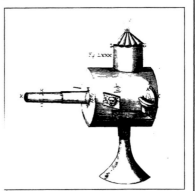

5

superimposed and animated onto translucent screens or directly onto smoke. Its iconography included human figures as well as unearthly spectres, often leading to the final apparition of a ghost.[14]

The 'covert' use of the lantern was also a strategy to circumvent the problem of weak lighting, which allowed only a short distance between the device and the screen. With the discovery of the oxyhydrogen limelight in the nineteenth century, the lantern could be placed at the back of the auditorium without obstructing the audience's view, therefore allowing front projections. Such progress in the field of illumination, together with the application of photography for the production of slides, marked the beginning of the popular 'overt' use of the magic lantern. The lantern became the mass medium of visual information, and lectures were performed to deliver moral, religious or propaganda content. Additionally, with the diffusion of the biunial (two lens) and triunial (three lens) lanterns, the showman was able to recreate the illusion of movement, either by fading between images using dissolving views slides, or by superimposing two slides, one on top of the other. These types of lanterns expanded the possibility of narrative construction, influencing those magicians and lanternists, such as George Méliès and George Albert Smith, who later turned to film.

'Twixt Two Worlds' sheds light on these chapters of the magic lantern's history, by displaying two 'improved phantasmagoria and dissolving views lanterns' (1860) from the Barnes Brothers' Collection in Turin, together with a biunial lantern (c.1850) from the Brighton and Hove Museums collections.[15] These devices marked a turning point in the transition between the still and the moving image, articulated here through the history of superimposition. A selection of magic lantern slides accompanies their display within the exhibition, since, as John Barnes recalls, 'a magic lantern without a collection of slides may not inappropriately be compared to a theatre without a scenery of actors.'[16] The selection includes hand-painted wooden lantern slides, photographic slides and digital animations developed from original sets of dissolving views, to encompass the wide range of visual effects that could be achieved through the magic lantern.[17]

OPPOSITE
New Magic Lantern Journal, Vol. 3., No. 3, October 1985. Courtesy Science Museum / Science & Society Picture Library

Phantasmagoria & dissolving view slide lanterns. From the Barnes Brothers Collection, National Cinema Museum, Turin. Courtesy Archives of the National Cinema Museum, Turin

14 Eric Barnouw, *The Magician and the Cinema*, Oxford University Press, Oxford, 1981.

15 Due to the vast success of the Phantasmagoria, a specific type of apparatus, initially introduced by Philip Carpenter, was named after the show.

16 John Barnes quotes James Martin's position in his article 'The Projected Image, A Short History of Magic Lantern Slides', *The New Magic Lantern Society Journal*, Vol.3, No.3, 1985, p.2.

17 The approach to the selection of slides has followed an iconographic criteria rather than an historical one, privileging those slides whose content and narrative more clearly resonate with the display's curatorial framework and experimenting with the possibility offered by digital technology to recreate and enhance some of these special effects.

George Albert Smith, *The Corsican Brothers*, 1898, black and white photographic postcard, 138 x 89 mm. From the Barnes Brothers Collection, Hove Museum. Courtesy Royal Pavilion and Museums, Brighton & Hove

OPPOSITE
Susan Hiller, *The Fight*, 2007. Purchased 2008. © Susan Hiller. Photo © Tate, London 2014

The introduction of the biunial lantern and the circulation of dissolving view slides encouraged the experimentation with double exposure and superimposition techniques in film. In his essay 'George Albert Smith's vision and transformations. The films of 1898', Frank Gray describes Smith's pioneering use of the 'vision scene' within his trick films. The vision scene was used to convey a different narrative plane and consisted of a second image constructed within a circular vignette and superimposed onto the main frame, either in the top-right- or top-left-hand side of the composition.[18] Before the introduction of separate shots, such a simple form of editing enabled a dialectical relationship between the main action in the central image, and a secondary action, which belonged to another spatial and temporal horizon. In 1898 Smith experimented with such techniques in several of his films. Of these, *Santa Claus* (1898) is perhaps the most delightful among the few that have survived. Inspired by Clement Moore's poem 'The Night Before Christmas', it shows two children who are waiting for the arrival of Santa Claus while in bed. Here the technique of the vision scene is used first to portray the appearance of Santa Claus in the children's dream, and subsequently his materialisation into the physical space of the children's room. From the vignette of the vision scene Santa Claus descends, through the chimney, into the film's main narrative plane.

Telepathic Instances

Smith made a remarkable contribution to the development of special effects in British cinema. Among the ephemera carefully assembled by the Barnes brothers, which today are part of the Brighton and Hove collection, is a postcard reminiscent of Smith's 1898 film *The Corsican Brothers*, another key example of his use of superimposition and the visual scene. The film was an adaptation of the play written by Dion Boucicault, a Victorian melodrama centred on the characters of twin brothers who were able to communicate via telepathy. The subject matter of the play strongly resonated with Smith's interest in telepathy and hypnosis that positioned him and his performances on the cusp between spiritualist practices and Victorian popular entertainment. Perhaps it raised the curiosity of the Barnes brothers too, who, as twins, sympathised with the notions of telepathy.[19]

18 Gray, op. cit.
19 The twins liked to recall when John opened the museum in St. Ives with his wife Carmen, Bill was at war, but nevertheless managed to send a telegram, which arrived exactly on the day of the opening, as per the result of a telepathic connection between them.

In the last decades of the twentieth century, a new wave of interest in spiritualism, telepathy and paranormal phenomena has permeated much contemporary art. This display reflects on whether the fascination with 'the other side' can be seen as an historical continuum that challenges, resists and surpasses a reading of the nineteenth century's history of media purely based on the transition from one technology to the next. In 'Twixt Two Worlds', the works of Susan Hiller (b.1940) and Jane and Louise Wilson (b.1967), included in the subsequent tour to the Towner in Eastbourne, are to be seen as critical interjections and interferences within the display's predominantly historical narrative.

Bodily Expressions
Susan Hiller's *The Fight* (2007) is a print of two boxing skeletons. The image is drawn from *An Entertainment* (1990) a four-screen video projection based on *Punch and Judy* shows, which were popular during the Victorian period. The print formally echoes the earliest-known representation of a moving slide for the magic lantern, which was sketched by Christiaan Huygens in his manuscripts from 1659.[20] It was an image of a skeleton removing its skull from its shoulders and replacing it while also moving its right arm. Such artificial recreation of motion was probably achieved through the superimposition of two sheets of glass: one fixed, representing the skeleton without the skull and perhaps without the right arm, and one movable, on which he painted the right arm and skull only.[21] Since the time of Huygens, the skeleton has played

20 Laurent Mannoni, *The Great Art of Light and Shadow: Archaeology of the Cinema*, Exeter Studies in Film History, Exeter, 2000.
21 Mannoni, op. cit., p.38.

Étienne-Jules Marey, Two photographic magic lantern slides, 11 x 8.5 cm. From the Muybridge Collection, Kingston Museum, London. Courtesy Kingston Museum and Heritage Service

FIG. 44.—This figure represents a trotting horse, furnished with the different experimental instruments; the horseman carrying the register of the pace. On the withers and the croup are instruments to show the reactions.

a key role in the iconography of the magic lantern and in the depiction of movement. Perhaps it is precisely because, as a symbol of death, it represents 'the negative' of the body and therefore the termination of movement, the quintessential bodily expression.

Not inadvertently, much of the study around movement that enabled the transition from the still to the moving image was famously carried out around the observation and representation of the body. By the second half of the nineteenth century the focus in photography shifted from the fixing of the image to fixing an instant of time through shorter exposures. Instantaneous photography could finally claim to 'seize a fraction of a second in a manner no human eye was capable of'.[22] Out of this fertile ground grew the experiments with chronophotography of the Anglo-American photographer Eadweard Muybridge (1830–1904) and French physiologist Étienne-Jules Marey (1830–1904), which opened up a new approach to the visualisation of movement of the body. The two men were acquainted with each other and their photographic experiments on human and animal locomotion had a long-lasting impact in the fields of both art and science.

Muybridge began his career as a professional photographer after a stagecoach accident that caused him neurological damage. He began photographing horses in 1872, exposing the images with a high-speed shutter built from a cigar box.[23] The dissatisfaction with his first results and the tumultuous events of his life – he is also known for having murdered his wife's lover – enhanced the fervour and obsession with which he returned to his horse sequences in 1877, in Palo Alto in California. The following year, while Muybridge released his first sequential photographs of moving horses, Marey published his major work *The Graphic Method*, advancing physics as his model of experimentation and using graphing instruments as tools to understand life processes, movement in particular, as mechanical processes.

Marey realised that the camera could render a concrete representation of all relationships that occur between one body part and the body as a whole at each phase of the movement.[24] During his experiment in the outdoor laboratory, the Station Physiologique in the Bois de Boulogne, he replaced a single camera for Muybridge's battery of cameras and then constructed a 'rapidly rotating slotted-disk shutter to briefly expose a single plate over and over again'.[25] Two remarkable sets of black and white photographic magic lantern slides from The Muybridge Collection at Kingston Museum document the background of these pivotal researches on movement. One set depicts the cameras and photographic tools used by Muybridge in Palo Alto, as he created the stage for his famous sequence of images. The other set is taken by Marey and illustrates a series of graphing instruments that could register the different paces of humans and horses in movement. Such graphic instruments, first designed and

22 Tom Gunning in Mannoni, op. cit.
23 Hollis Frampton, 'Eadweard Muybridge, Fragments of a Tesseract', in *On the Camera Arts and Consecutive Matters: The Writings of Hollis Frampton*, MIT Press, Boston, 2009.
24 Marta Braun and E. Whitcombe, 'Marey, Muybridge, and Londe: The Photography of Pathological Locomotion', *History of Photography*, Vol.23, No.3, 1999, p.220.
25 Braun and Whitcombe, op. cit., p.222.

implemented by Marey, are the ancestors of modern medical instruments that are still in use in hospitals today.[26]

The study of the movement of the human body successfully pioneered by Marey and Muybridge found a concrete application in the field of medicine, and specifically in the practice of psychiatric photography, which developed during the second half of the nineteenth century. The significant body of work produced by the photographer Albert Londe (1858–1917) sits at this particularly interesting juncture between art and science. Londe was a friend and colleague of Marey, who worked at the Salpêtrière Hospital in Paris for the most famous clinician of the time, Jean-Martin Charcot (1825–93). Charcot used hypnotism as a method of experimentation on living subjects and conducted extensive photographic studies on his hysterical patients. These are all gathered in the book *The Iconographie photographique de la Salpêtrière (1876–79)*, a record of his ambiguous clinical method, which 'went so far as to treat his patients *as* photographs'.[27] It was around the study of hysteria that Sigmund Freud (1856–1939) famously distanced himself from the work of Charcot, who was his mentor at the Salpêtrière Hospital. In 1895 Freud proposed a new understanding of hysteria that was rooted in unconscious conflicts rather than fragile nerves or sexual disturbance, linking the symptoms of the

NOUVELLE ICONOGRAPHIE DE LA SALPÊTRIÈRE — T. III. PL. XVIII

PHOTOTYPE NÉGATIF A. LONDE — PHOTOCOLLOGRAPHIE CHÊNE & LONGUET

BAILLEMENTS HYSTÉRIQUES

LECROSNIER & BABÉ, ÉDITEURS

26 These include oscilliscopes, electrocardiographs, encephalographs. See Braun and Whitcombe, op. cit., p.219.

27 Braun and Whitcombe, op. cit., p.222.

body with the (in)ability of memory to process traumatic events that were too painful to be expressed.

Much like the images of ghosts and skeletons, the figure of the hysterical woman has haunted the social imagination since Victorian times. In Douglas Gordon's work *Hysterical* (1995), included in the display's tour to the Towner, this figure returns in the artist's investigation of bodily movements and psychic disturbance within the expanded space of cinema. This two-screen video installation takes the viewer back to the beginning of the century and to the treatment of hysteria challenged by Charcot and Freud. It is based on archival footage drawn from a 1908 scientific film made by Turin-based film pioneer Roberto Omegna. The footage that Gordon appropriated features a woman, in the midst of hysterical convulsion, whose face is masked to hide her identity, being lowered to a bed by two male figures, a professor and an assistant. Gordon's installation comprises a rear projection in which the footage appears on two large freestanding screens. The same section of footage is projected at different speeds, in a loop, on each of the screens, producing a mirror effect. Gordon's work gives form to the notion of the double: hysteria and early cinema are visually and spatially rendered as split identities across two different time frames.

Swallowing the Image

Such an identity split not only reiterates cinema's origins in both science and magic, but also provokes a critical reflection on the long-lasting relationship between the still and the moving image brilliantly captured by *The Big Swallow (A Photographic Contortion)* – a 1901 silent comedy by British film pioneer James Williamson (1855–1933). In the film, a man is physically irritated by the presence of a photographer; he yells at him, chases him away, moves nervously while swinging a stick in sign of protest, and eventually solves the problem by swallowing him and his camera whole. While the photographer appears lost in the concavity of the man's throat, the latter winks at the audience with contentment. Cinema swallowed photography: it could not fight it, nor exorcise it. With a decisive gesture of appropriation, cinema transformed the irresistible realism of the photographic image into the pre-condition for its fantastic narratives. In the words of André Bazin, 'cinema owes to photography the dissolution of all forced oppositions between the world of reality and the world of dreams, as one is unconceivable without the other.'[28]

28 André Bazin, 'The Life and Death of Superimposition (1946)', *Film-Philosophy Journal*, Vol.6, No.1, 2002

James
Williamson,
*The Big
Swallow*, 1901,
35mm, black
and white,
silent. Film
stills courtesy
BFI National
Archive

Display 1

Nothing Beautiful Unless Useful

Curatorial Fellow: Anna Colin

Host venue: The Harris Museum and Art Gallery, Preston

Tour venue: Victoria Gallery and Museum, University of Liverpool 7 March – 31 May 2014

L.S. Lowry
The Bandstand, Peel Park, Salford, 1931
Oil on canvas
43.2 × 62.2 cm
York Museums Trust (York Art Gallery)

Sir Frank Brangwyn
Industrial Landscape, c.1920
Lithograph
54.5 × 75 cm
Harris Museum & Art Gallery, Preston

Edward Alexander Wadsworth
Netherton Furnaces, 1919
Watercolour, ink, pencil
15.9 × 25.6 cm
Manchester City Galleries

Marion Rhodes
Yorkshire Landscape, Looking Towards Halifax from Lindley Moor, date unknown
Etching, paper
41 × 51 cm
Kirklees Collection: Huddersfield Art Gallery

Manchester Art Museum

Ancoats – General View from Victoria Hall Roof, c.1895
Reproduction of photograph
Date unknown
Courtesy of Manchester Libraries, Information and Archives, Manchester City Council

G.E. Anderton
Ancoats Old Hall, c. 1900
Reproduction of photograph
Date unknown
Courtesy of Manchester Libraries, Information and Archives, Manchester City Council

G.E. Anderton
Ancoats Hall, Horsfall Museum (Manchester Art Gallery)
Date unknown
Facsimile

G.E. Anderton
A Plan of the Manchester Art Museum at Ancoats Hall
Date unknown
Facsimile

G.E. Anderton
Monday Popular Lectures
Date unknown
Facsimile

John Ruskin
Dead Bittern, 1900
Watercolour
29 × 49.5 cm
Abbot Hall Art Gallery, Lakeland Arts Trust, Kendal, Cumbria

John Ruskin
Near Interlaken, 1870
Pencil, ink, watercolour and body colour
15 × 24.2 cm
Abbot Hall Art Gallery, Lakeland Arts Trust, Kendal, Cumbria

John Ruskin
Clouds on Mountain, Martigny, date unknown
Watercolour
12.2 × 20 cm
Abbot Hall Art Gallery, Lakeland Arts Trust, Kendal, Cumbria

John Ruskin
Chamouni, Mont Blanc de St. Gervais, 1849
Pencil, watercolour and body colour
14.2 × 22.2 cm
Abbot Hall Art Gallery, Lakeland Arts Trust, Kendal, Cumbria

William Holman Hunt
Afternoon (Study: Sunset), 1883
Watercolour and body colour
17.6 × 12.6 cm
Manchester City Galleries

James Hamilton Hay
Wave, c.1912–14
Oil on canvas
2.5 × 76.2 × 81 cm
Williamson Art Gallery & Museum, Birkenhead; Wirral Museums Service

J. Gould & W. Hart
Monograph of the Paradiseidae; Craspedophora Magnifica, 1891–98
Ink and watercolour
55.5 × 37 cm
Manchester City Galleries

J. Gould & W. Hart
Monograph of the Paradiseidae; Rhipidornis Gulielmi, III, 1891–98
Ink and watercolour
54.4 × 37 cm
Manchester City Galleries

Emily Gertrude Thomson
Stellaria, 1882
Watercolour on paper
26.5 × 18.8 cm
Manchester City Galleries

Emily Gertrude Thomson
Forget-me-not, 1882
Watercolour on paper
26.4 × 18.8 cm
Manchester City Galleries

Walter Crane
Design for The Workers' Union, Manchester District, 1890
Pencil, pen and ink, watercolour and gouache
25.4 × 23.4 cm
Whitworth Art Gallery, The University of Manchester

Jeffrey & Co. after Walter Crane
Orange Tree, 1902
Wallpaper, colour print from woodblocks
156.8 × 106 cm
Whitworth Art Gallery, The University of Manchester

Ford Madox Brown
Study for the Oil Painting Work 1852/6 (Compositional Study), c.1856
Watercolour on paper
19.7 × 28 cm
Manchester City Galleries

Edward Burne-Jones
Study of Hands for 'King Cophetua and the Beggar Maid', c.1883
Pencil on paper
23.2 × 17.9 cm
Manchester City Galleries

Unknown
Gwladys Rogers at work, date unknown
Photograph
11 × 16 cm
Peter Scott Gallery, Live at LICA, Lancaster University

Gwladys Rogers
Pilkington Pot, 1910
Ceramic
5 × 6.5 × 6.5 cm
Peter Scott Gallery, Live at
LICA, Lancaster University

Gordon Forsyth
Pilkington Pot, 1912
Ceramic
13 × 13 × 13 cm
Peter Scott Gallery, Live at
LICA, Lancaster University

Richard Joyce
Pilkington Pot, 1915
Ceramic
12 × 16 × 12 cm
Peter Scott Gallery, Live at
LICA, Lancaster University

Gwladys Rogers
Pilkington Pot, 1930
Ceramic
15.5 × 16 × 15.5 cm
Peter Scott Gallery, Live at
LICA, Lancaster University

Walter Crane
Pilkington Pot, 1905
Ceramic
13 × 16.5 × 13 cm
Peter Scott Gallery, Live at
LICA, Lancaster University

Gordon Forsyth
Pilkington Pot, 1908
Ceramic
25 × 31.5 × 25 cm
Peter Scott Gallery, Live at
LICA, Lancaster University

Crayfish, Undated
Ivory carving
10 × 20 × 40 cm
Grundy Art Gallery,
Blackpool, Samuel Bancroft
Bequest

Acorns, Undated
Ivory carving
3 × 3 × 4 cm
Grundy Art Gallery,
Blackpool, Samuel Bancroft
Bequest

Banana, Undated
Ivory carving
5 × 5 × 15 cm
Grundy Art Gallery,
Blackpool, Samuel Bancroft
Bequest

Two figs, Undated
Ivory carving
5 × 5 × 5 cm
Grundy Art Gallery,
Blackpool, Samuel Bancroft
Bequest

Harry James Powell
Vase, 1878
Opalescent blue glass
12.1 × 6.2 × 6.2 cm
Manchester City Galleries

Harry James Powell
Vase, c.1888
Pale yellow-green and milky-
white glass straw opal vase
16 × 7.3 × 7.3 cm
Manchester City Galleries

Harry James Powell
Bowl, c.1888
Opalescent blue opal glass
5.7 × 11.2 × 11.2 cm
Manchester City Galleries

Harry James Powell
Vase, c.1888
Opalescent coloured glass,
blue opal
16.5 × 7.2 × 7.2 cm
Manchester City Galleries

Harry James Powell
Vase, 1877
Straw opal glass
16.4 × 11 × 11 cm
Manchester City Galleries

John Ruskin
Lily, date unknown
Engraved block
7.2 × 5.8 cm
Manchester City Galleries

John Ruskin
Aiguille Charmox, c.1856
Pen and watercolour on wood
13.5 × 12.5 cm
Manchester City Galleries

John Ruskin
Aiguille Du Midi, France,
c.1850–55
Pen and black ink and
watercolour on wood
11.5 × 18.8 cm
Manchester City Galleries

John Ruskin
Flower, date unknown
Engraved block
5.8 × 10.2 cm
Manchester City Galleries

Leeds Arts Club

Jacob Kramer
Abstract Composition, c.1917
Gouache on paper
29.5 × 22.5 cm
Leeds Museums and Galleries
(Leeds Art Gallery)

Jacob Kramer
Abstract Study, c.1917
Watercolour on paper
25.1 × 35.7 cm
Leeds Museums and Galleries
(Leeds Art Gallery)

Jacob Kramer
Industrial Landscape, 1914
Drawing
35.5 × 44.1 cm
Leeds Museums and Galleries
(Leeds Art Gallery)

Sir William Rothenstein
Portrait of WB Yeats, 1916
Black lead, paper
38.7 × 28.3 cm
Leeds Museums and Galleries
(Leeds Art Gallery)

Emily Ford
Miss Josephine Butler, 1903
Black chalk heightened with
white
50 × 39.8 cm
Leeds Museums and Galleries
(Leeds Art Gallery)

Emily Ford
Study for a Mural, date
unknown
Drawing
64.1 × 22.3 cm
Leeds Museums and Galleries
(Leeds Art Gallery)

Eric Gill
The Skaters, 1897–1933
Line engraving
13.4 × 13.4 cm
Leeds Museums and Galleries
(Leeds Art Gallery)

Eric Gill
*Christ and the Money
Changers,* c.1919
Ink, paper
7.4 × 8.5 cm
Leeds Museums and Galleries
(Leeds Art Gallery)

Mass Observation

Humphrey Spender
*Inside 85 Davenport Street,
planning day's activities,*
1937–8/2013
Photograph
43.5 × 53.5 cm, framed
From the Collection
of Bolton Library and
Museum Services

Graham Bell
*Graham Bell's Mass
Observation sketch book,* 1938
Sketchbook
23 × 18 cm
From the Collection
of Bolton Library and
Museum Services

Tom Binks (Day Survey
Respondent: 217)
*Mass Observation Day
Survey Extract,* 1937
Facsimile
22.9 × 17.8 cm
The Mass Observation
Archive, University of
Sussex

Humphrey Spender
Street Accident, 1937–8
43.5 × 53.5 cm, framed
From the Collection
of Bolton Library and
Museum Services

Humphrey Spender
*Election campaign –
announcement van,* 1937–8
43.5 × 53.5 cm, framed
From the Collection
of Bolton Library and
Museum Services

Humphrey Spender
*By-election polling day:
Going to vote,* 1937–8
43.5 × 53.5 cm, framed
From the Collection
of Bolton Library and
Museum Services

Humphrey Spender
*Parliamentary by-election
– children hanging around
outside,* 1937–8/2013
43.5 × 53.5 cm, framed
From the Collection
of Bolton Library and
Museum Services

Humphrey Spender
Town centre pub interior –
drinking, smoking, dominoes,
1937–8
53.5 × 43.5 cm, framed
From the Collection
of Bolton Library and
Museum Services

Humphrey Spender
Scrubbing and whitening
pavement, 1937–8
43.5 × 53.5 cm, framed
From the Collection
of Bolton Library and
Museum Services

Humphrey Spender
On the roof of Bolton Art
Gallery, Mere Hall: William
Coldstream's painting,
1937–8/2013
43.5 × 53.5 cm, framed
From the Collection
of Bolton Library and
Museum Services

Humphrey Spender
Ashington miners' art
group, 1937–8
43.5 × 53.5 cm, framed
From the Collection
of Bolton Library and
Museum Services

Humphrey Spender
Pub scene – landlord very
hostile, 1937–8
43.5 × 53.5 cm, framed
From the Collection
of Bolton Library and
Museum Services

Humphrey Spender
Children peeping through
hole in fence, 1937–8
53.5 × 43.5 cm, framed
From the Collection
of Bolton Library and
Museum Services

Humphrey Spender
Ashington – washing in road
between terraced houses,
1937–8
43.5 × 53.5 cm, framed
From the Collection
of Bolton Library and
Museum Services

Humphrey Jennings
Spare Time, 1939
35mm, transferred to DVD
15 minutes
Courtesy of the BFI

The Cotton Museum

Charles E. Shaw
The Yellow Factory 'One of
the First Mills by Sir John
Horrocks', 1852
Pencil, ink and wash on paper
12 × 9 cm
Harris Museum & Art
Gallery, Preston

Patti Mayor
The Half-Timer, 1906–8
Oil on canvas
86.7 × 61.4 cm
Harris Museum & Art
Gallery, Preston

Unknown
Mr. Large Firm, 1854
Engraving hand-tinted
with ink & watercolour
23.5 × 33 cm
With permission from
Lancashire Archives and
The Lancashire Evening Post

Unknown
Recruiting Sergeant, 1854
Engraving hand-tinted
with ink & watercolour
23.8 × 33 cm
With permission from
Lancashire Archives and
The Lancashire Evening Post

Unknown
Warping and Winding, 1854
Engraving hand-tinted with
ink & watercolour
23.8 × 54.6 cm
With permission from
Lancashire Archives and
The Lancashire Evening Post

Unknown
Mixing Room, 1854
Engraving hand-tinted
with ink & watercolour
54.6 × 54.9 cm
With permission from
Lancashire Archives and
The Lancashire Evening Post

Unknown
The Devil Room, 1854
Engraving hand-tinted
with ink & watercolour
23.8 × 54.9 cm
With permission from
Lancashire Archives and
The Lancashire Evening Post

William Henry Hunt
Peaches, Grapes, Redcurrants
and Strawberries Against
a Mossy Bank, c.1860
Watercolour and gouache
on paper
41 × 51 cm
Harris Museum & Art
Gallery, Preston

Henry J. Wells
Portrait of Thomas Miller Jnr.,
1863
Pencil and wash on paper,
leather case
31 × 54 × 3 cm
Harris Museum & Art
Gallery, Preston

Cecil Musk
Queen Cotton, 1941
(Release Year)
Technicolour Film
13 min. 49 sec.
British Council Film
Collection

Horrockses Cotton
Transformation Display,
c.1905
Wooden display box
containing cotton samples
59 × 48.5 × 9.8 cm
Harris Museum &
Art Gallery, Preston

Amalgamated Cotton
Mills Trust Limited
Concerning Cotton, 1920
Book (open)
29 × 22.5 × 4 cm
Harris Museum &
Art Gallery, Preston

Amalgamated Cotton
Mills Trust Limited
Concerning Cotton, 1920
Book (closed)
29 × 22.5 × 4 cm
Lancashire Archives

Unknown
Machines, 1930s
Photograph
15 × 15 cm
With permission from
Lancashire Archives
and Coates PLC

Unknown
Hairnet Lady, 1930s
Photograph
15 × 15 cm
With permission from
Lancashire Archives
and Coates PLC

Unknown
Piles of Material, 1930s
Photograph
15 × 15 cm
With permission from
Lancashire Archives
and Coates PLC

Horrocks, Crewdson
& Company Preston
Pattern books of Horrocks,
Crewdson & Company,
Preston, 1940–50s
Pattern books
6.4 × 38.1 × 27.9 cm
With permission from
Lancashire Archives
and Coates PLC

Unknown
The Cotton Lords of Preston,
c.1854
Printout of ballad sheet
42 × 29.7 cm
Reproduced by kind
permission of the
Syndics of Cambridge
University Library

Display 2

**Damn braces:
Bless relaxes**

Curatorial Fellow:
Helen Kaplinsky

Host venue:
Ferens Art
Gallery, Hull

Tour venue:
mima,
Middlesbrough
11 April–
27 June 2014

An Act for Dividing and Inclosing the open and common fields, common meadows, lammas grounds and other commonable lands and grounds, in the Parish of Fotherby in the County of Lincoln, 1764
Paper
32 × 21.5 cm
The Museum of
Lincolnshire Life

Illustrations to the Book of Job invented and engraved by William Blake, London, 1825
On fly-leaf 'Alfred Tennyson, Farringford, Freshwater, I.W.' [Isle of Wight]
The Tennyson Research
Centre, Lincolnshire
County Council

J. Brown after Thomas H. Hair
Newcastle upon Tyne, undated
Engraving.
Laing Art Gallery,
Newcastle upon Tyne
(Tyne & Wear Archives
& Museums)

Richard Brown
Kett's Castle , Norwich,
1824
Engraving on paper
10.9 × 15.8 cm
Norfolk Museums &
Archaeology Service
(Norwich Castle
Museum & Art Gallery)

Heath Bunting
_readme.html (Own, Be Owned or Remain Invisible), 1998
Online text linked with URLs
irational.org/_readme
Presented as online website

Heath Bunting
Isolation in Velocity: Speed Inducing Street Graphics,
1995
irational.org/heath/velocity
Presented as online website
Commissioned by Hull Time
Based Arts for Root Festival
'95: Civil Liberties Civic Pride

Heath Bunting
Skint – The Internet Beggar,
1996
Online form for credit-
card transfers
irational.org/skint
Presented as online website
Commissioned by Hull Time
Based Arts for Root Festival
'96: Skint

Rachel Baker and
Heath Bunting
Routeless, 1997
Presented as online website
irational.org/routeless
Commissioned by Hull Time
Based Arts for Root Festival
'97: Rootless

Ralph Hedley Charlton
Gypsies Camped on the Beach, near South Shields, 1876
Oil on canvas
41 × 54 cm
South Shields Museum &
Art Gallery, South Shields

Ralph Hedley Charlton
Billy Purvis Stealing the Bundle, 1876
Watercolour on paper
26.8 × 22.6 cm
Laing Art Gallery,
Newcastle upon Tyne
(Tyne & Wear Archives
& Museums)

John Constable
Cloud Study, 1821
Oil on paper, pasted
onto oak panel
23 × 30.2 cm
Ferens Art Gallery,
Hull Museums

Corn dolly
Large wheat
28 × 9.5 cm
Made by William Blake
of Barton Turf, 1947
Norfolk Museums &
Archaeology Service
(Norwich Castle Museum
& Art Gallery)

Corn dolly
Small wheat
21 × 5 cm
Made by William Blake
of Barton Turf, 1947
Norfolk Museums &
Archaeology Service
(Norwich Castle Museum
& Art Gallery)

Corn dolly
Barley
31 × 11 cm
Made by William Blake
of Barton Turf, 1947
Norfolk Museums &
Archaeology Service
(Norwich Castle Museum
& Art Gallery)

Edward 'Ned' Corvan
Billy Purvis Stealing a Bundle,
1855
Oil on canvas
46 × 61 cm
Laing Art Gallery,
Newcastle upon Tyne
(Tyne & Wear Archives
& Museums)

Facsimile of pencil and
watercolour drawing
of *Kett's Castle, Norwich c. 1809–1810/Ketts Hill, Norwich*
by John Sell Cotman
22.1 × 31.5 cm
Norfolk Museums &
Archaeology Service
(Norwich Castle Museum
& Art Gallery)

Facsimile of pencil and
watercolour drawing of
Mousehold Heath, Norwich , c.1810/Heath Scene
by John Sell Cotman
30.3 × 46.4 cm
Norfolk Museums &
Archaeology Service
(Norwich Castle
Museum & Art Gallery)

John Joseph Cotman
Dredger, undated
Chalk on paper
24.5 × 32.2 cm
Norfolk Museums &
Archaeology Service
(Norwich Castle
Museum & Art Gallery)

John Sell Cotman
Kett's Castle Norwich, c.1809–1810/Ketts Hill, Mousehold Heath, Norwich (c.1807), 1809–1810
Drawing
8.4 × 13 cm
Norfolk Museums & Archaeology Service (Norwich Castle Museum & Art Gallery)

Fran Cottell
A Meeting Outside Time, 1988
Mixed media, including photographs, slides, archive material, relating to performance in Northumberland National Park.
Commissioned by New Work Newcastle '88 in association with Edge '88.
Supported by Projects UK, Northumberland National Park, Laing Art Gallery, Tyne and Wear Museum Services, Newcastle City Council, Northern Arts, Arts Council and Riverside.
Map of Newcastle:
Photo by Verdi Yahooda
Contact sheet and b/w photographs: Karen Melvin.
Collection of the artist

Fran Cottell
A Meeting Outside Time, 1988
Audio recording
Contributors:
Helen Cadwallader, Rachel Chapman, Lynda Mellor, Vicky Ramshaw, Caroline Taylor, Liz Todd, Kate Tregaskis, Eileen Tunney, Vicky Winter.
Commissioned by New Work Newcastle '88 in association with Edge '88.
Supported by Projects UK, Northumberland National Park, Laing Art Gallery, Tyne and Wear Museum Services, Newcastle City Council, Northern Arts, Arts Council and Riverside.
Collection of the artist

Peter DeWint
Lincolnshire Landscape (Near Horncastle), c.1813–26
Oil on canvas
107 × 171 cm
The Collection: Art and Archaeology in Lincolnshire (Usher Gallery, Lincoln) Purchased with the assistance of the Art Fund, 194

Peter DeWint
A Ruined Wall, undated
Grey and white chalk and grey paper
22.2 × 28.7 cm
The Collection: Art and Archaeology in Lincolnshire (Usher Gallery, Lincoln)

Peter DeWint
Exchequergate, Lincoln, c.1815
Watercolour on paper
45.7 × 50.8 cm
The Collection: Art and Archaeology in Lincolnshire (Usher Gallery, Lincoln)

Peter DeWint
Landscape with Cows, c.1815–20
Watercolour on paper
19 × 27 cm
The Collection: Art and Archaeology in Lincolnshire (Usher Gallery, Lincoln)

Thomas H. Hair
Broomside Colliery, 1835
Watercolour on paper
23 × 35 cm
Hatton Gallery, Newcastle University (Tyne & Wear Archives & Museums)

Thomas H. Hair
Pemberton Main Colliery, c.1835–39
Watercolour on paper
23 × 35 cm
Hatton Gallery, Newcastle University (Tyne & Wear Archives & Museums)

Thomas H. Hair
Gosforth Colliery, c.1835–39
Watercolour on paper
c.21 × 31 cm
Hatton Gallery, Newcastle University (Tyne & Wear Archives & Museums)

Thomas H. Hair
Airshaft, Wallsend, 1839
Watercolour on paper
23 × 36.5 cm
Hatton Gallery, Newcastle University (Tyne & Wear Archives & Museums)

F. Howard
Sketchers Manual,
Printed in 1837 with inscription 'This valuable little work presented to J.J. Cotman by his Father' and sketch insert of marine subject by John Sell Cotman on flyleaf 21 August 1839
23 × 30 × 2.5 cm
Norfolk Museums & Archaeology Service (Norwich Castle Museum & Art Gallery)

Oliver Laric
The Lincoln 3D Scans Project, 2013
Wallpaper
The Collection and Usher Gallery, Lincoln

Nineteenth century copy of 1589 map of Mousehold Heath, Norwich
A trewe discripcon of Mushold heath together with the close made in and upon the said heath
59 × 43 cm
Norfolk Museums & Archaeology Service (Norwich Castle Museum & Art Gallery)

Paul Nash
The Rye Marshes, 1932
Oil on canvas
54.5 × 98 cm
Ferens Art Gallery, Hull Museums

Grayson Perry
Untitled (A man wearing a bowler hat and holding a gun stands next to a hunt post), 2006
Photograph
60 × 42 cm
The Collection: Art and Archaeology in Lincolnshire (Usher Gallery, Lincoln) Gift from the Victoria Miro Gallery

Grayson Perry
Untitled (Two figures standing over a child's coffin), 2006
Photograph
60 × 42 cm
The Collection: Art and Archaeology in Lincolnshire (Usher Gallery, Lincoln) Gift from the Victoria Miro Gallery

Simon Poulter
Be Realistic – Market the Impossible (Counter Marketing series), 1996
Poster
151.5 × 101 cm
Commissioned by Hull Time Based Arts for Root Festival '96: Skint
Courtesy University of Bristol Theatre Collection
© Simon Poulter

Simon Poulter
Hull – European Gateway, UK Ltd (Propaganda series), 1995
Poster
59.5 × 42 cm
Commissioned by Hull Time Based Arts for Root Festival '95: Civil Liberties Civic Pride
Collection of Helen Kaplinsky
© Simon Poulter

Simon Poulter
Counter Marketing (Year of Skint Root Festival), 1996
Propaganda booklet and five inserts
Commissioned by Hull Time Based Arts for Root Festival '96: Skint.
Courtesy University of Bristol Theatre Collection
© Simon Poulter

Simon Poulter
UK Ltd (Part of Propaganda Series) Privatise Stonehenge Press Release, 1995
UK Ltd (Part of Propaganda Series) Privatise Stonehenge Marketing Material, 1995
UK Ltd (Part of Propaganda Series) Privatise Stonehenge Share Offer, 1995
UK Ltd (Part of Propaganda series) UK Ltd Press Release, 1995
UK Ltd (Part of Propaganda series) A Real Power Issue Press Release, 1995

UK Ltd (Part of Propaganda series) Is it Art or Propaganda? Press Release, 1995
UK Ltd (Part of Propaganda series) Design for Advertising Campaign 1, 1995
UK Ltd (Part of Propaganda series) Design for Advertising Campaign 2, 1995
Commissioned by Hull Time Based Arts for Root Festival '95: Civil Liberties Civic Pride.
Courtesy University of Bristol Theatre Collection
© Simon Poulter

Sir Francis Job Short after Turner
Solway Moss, Cattle Drovers, 1887
Mezzotint, paper and sepia ink
18.2 × 26.6 cm
Gainsborough Old Hall, Lincolnshire County Council

James Stark
Kett's Castle, undated
Engraving on paper
11.8 × 16.6 cm
Norfolk Museums & Archaeology Service (Norwich Castle Museum & Art Gallery)

Alfred Tennyson
In Memoriam A.H.H,
MS Notebook known as 'The Butcher's Book', 1842–48
36.5 × 18 cm (open)
The Tennyson Research Centre, Lincolnshire County Council

Northern Farmer Old Style, 1864
Read by Edward Campion and recorded in 1969. New recording produced by The Society for Lincolnshire History and Archaeology, 2009
The Tennyson Research Centre, Lincolnshire County Council

Display 3

The Best is Not Too Good for You

Curatorial Fellow: Ingrid Swenson

Host venue: Wolverhampton Art Gallery

Tour venue: Rugby Art Gallery & Museum
28 June– 30 August 2014

Posset pot, maker's initials IB and RF
1696, Staffordshire
Earthenware, decorated in coloured slips
15 × 28 × 22 cm
The Potteries Museum & Art Gallery, Stoke-on-Trent

The Handmade Vessel

David Leach
Fluted Bowl
Before 1963, Leach Pottery, Cornwall
Stoneware
14.3 × 18.5cm
Collection of the Herbert Art Gallery & Museum, Coventry

Small dish with pair of fishes design, c.1050–1127
Ding ware
White Porcelain
2.2 × 12 cm
Collection of the Herbert Art Gallery & Museum, Coventry

Gwyn Hanssen Piggot
Bowl, undated
Stoneware
7.3 × 11.3 × 11.3 cm
University of Warwick Art Collection

Small bowl, 224–651 AD
Sassanian dynasty Persia
Ceramic with turquoise glaze
4.8 × 9.3 × 9.3 cm
New Art Gallery Walsall

Jug, undated
Winchcombe Pottery, Gloucestershire
Stoneware
20.5 × 15 × 18.5 cm
University of Warwick Art Collection

Lucie Rie
Bowl, undated
Porcelain, yellow glaze
17.4 × 9.2 cm
Leicester Arts and Museums Service

Katherine Pleydell-Bouverie
Small vessel, 1935
Stoneware, green glaze
8.5 × 10 × 10 cm
Nottingham City Museums & Galleries

Bowl, 1908
Ruskin Pottery, West Midlands
Stoneware, yellow glazed
11 × 24 cm
Nottingham City Museums & Galleries

Patrick Caulfield
Pink Jug, 1981
Screenprint, edition of 80
98.5 × 80 cm
University of Warwick Art Collection

Politics, Protest and Civil Rights

Mug commemorating 'The People's March for Jobs', 1981
Stoneware
9.4 × 10.3 cm
Collection of the Herbert Art Gallery & Museum, Coventry

Jug with Portrait of Francis Burdett
Early-nineteenth century, Staffordshire
Earthenware, transfer-printed
14 × 15 × 13 cm
Nottingham City Museums & Galleries

Teapot, with poem 'The Absent Minded Beggar' by Rudyard Kipling, illustration by Carlton Woodville
C.1899–1901, Staffordshire
Earthenware, transfer-printed
10.4 × 19.8 × 12.2 cm
Leicester Arts and Museums Service

Jug in support of 'Caroline our much injured Queen'
C.1820, Staffordshire
Earthenware, transfer-printed and hand-decorated
10 × 13.5 × 9.5 cm
The Potteries Museum & Art Gallery, Stoke-on-Trent

Anti-slavery medallion, 'Am I Not a Man and A Brother?', 1795, Modelled by William Hackwood, Wedgwood
Ceramic
3.5 × 3.1 cm
Courtesy of the Wedgewood Museum Trust, Barlaston

Tithe pig group, eighteenth century
Derby
Porcelain, hand-painted
15 × 13 × 8 cm
Nottingham City Museums & Galleries

Tile depicting the Boston Massachusetts Memorial, c.1877, Wedgwood, Staffordshire
Earthenware, transfer-printed
15 × 15 × 1 cm
Leicester Arts and Museums Service

Paul Scott
Cockle Pickers cup and saucer, 2007
In-glaze decal collages with gold on Royal Copenhagen saucer, and pearlware cup (c.1780)
8.5 × 13.5 cm
Courtesy of the artist

Uncle Tom, c.1852
Earthenware
22 × 8.5 × 6 cm
The Potteries Museum & Art Gallery, Stoke-on-Trent purchased with grant in aid from the V&A, London, The Art Fund and the Friends of the Potteries Museum & Art Gallery, Stoke-on-Trent

Teapot, 'Have a cup of tea in peace', 1919
Bargeware, Derbyshire
Earthenware
16.5 × 23 × 13 cm
Nottingham City Museums & Galleries

Figure of John Brown (attributed to Sampson Smith, Staffordshire), c.1859
Earthenware
35 x 17.5 x 7.5 cm
The Potteries Museum & Art Gallery, Stoke-on-Trent

Joe Tilson
Ho Chi Minh, 1970
Screenprint collage
145 × 90 cm
Wolverhampton Art Gallery & Museums

Richard Hamilton
Kent State, 1970
Screenprint on paper, edition of 5,000
67.2 × 87.2 cm
University of Warwick Art Collection

Andy Warhol
Birmingham Race Riot, 1964
Screenprint on paper, edition of 500
50.9 × 61.0 cm
University of Warwick Art Collection

Trade and Industry

Jug, 'Success to the Weavers' Early-nineteenth century, Staffordshire
Earthenware, transfer-printed and sgraffitoed
14 × 15.8 cm
Collection of the Herbert Art Gallery & Museum, Coventry

Paul Scott
Spode Closed Shop, 2009/11
In-glaze decals and gold lustre on salvaged Spode bone china plate collected from closed factory
1.5 × 31 cm
Courtesy of the artist

Christine Borland
Family Conversation Piece, 1999
Bone china with blue ship design in Delftware style
Dimensions variable
Leamington Spa Art Gallery & Museum (Warwick District Council)

Childs's mug 'Industry – Learn to Live', c.1840
Lusterware with beehive motif
6 × 6.5 cm
Nottingham City Museums & Galleries

Plate celebrating Queen Victoria's Jubilee, 1887
Earthenware, transfer-printed
28 cm
Leamington Spa Art Gallery & Museum (Warwick District Council)

Richard Hamilton
Five Tyres Remoulded, 1972
Screenprint on paper, edition of 40
81.3 × 55.9 cm
Wolverhampton Art Gallery & Museums

Humour and Satire

Jug, 'John Bull shewing the Corsican Monkey!!' 1802–1808, Staffordshire
Earthenware with pearlware glaze
18.5 × 21 × 16 cm
Nottingham City Museums & Galleries

Bear jug, 1812
Staffordshire
Earthenware
26 × 21 × 12 cm
Nottingham City Museums & Galleries

Toby jug in the shape of Gordon Brown
c.2005, modelled by Ray Noble for Bairstow Manor, Staffordshire
Earthenware
22 × 13 × 20 cm
The Potteries Museum & Art Gallery, Stoke-on-Trent

Teapot and cover in the form of Margaret Thatcher, Late 1980s
Designed by Fluck and Law for Carlton Ware
Earthenware
22 × 28 × 15 cm
The Potteries Museum & Art Gallery, Stoke-on-Trent purchased with grant in aid from the V&A, London, The Art Fund and the Friends of the Potteries Museum & Art Gallery, Stoke-on-Trent

Grayson Perry
Video installation, 1999
Earthenware
28 × 14 × 14 cm
The Potteries Museum & Art Gallery, Stoke-on-Trent Purchased through the Contemporary Art Society Special Collection Scheme with Lottery funding from Arts Council England, 2000

Potato-shaped flask, 1800–1830, Staffordshire
Earthenware
16.6 × 9 × 5.9 cm
Leicester Arts and Museums Service

Mug commemorating Prince Charles's engagement to Lady Diana Spencer, 1982
Illustrated by Marc for Carlton Ware
Stoneware, transfer-printed
9 × 8 × 11 cm
Nottingham City Museums & Galleries

Mug commemorating the birth of Prince George, 2013
Illustration by Steve Bell, edition 300
Stoneware, transfer-printed
9 x 8 × 11 cm
Collection of Ingrid Swenson

Mug, *A Lady's Maid Purchasing a Leek,* Late-eighteenth century
Earthenware, transfer-printed
13 × 12 × 8 cm
Nottingham City Museums & Galleries

The Roles of Women

Anya Gallaccio
While Reaching for Alma Ata, 2003
Slip-cast porcelain
Dimensions variable
The Potteries Museum & Art Gallery, Stoke-on-Trent Purchased through the Contemporary Art Society Special Collection Scheme with Lottery funding from Arts Council England, 2005

Figure of Venus, c.1790–1797,
Wedgwood, Staffordshire
Earthenware
16 × 8 × 5 cm
The Potteries Museum &
Art Gallery, Stoke-on-Trent
Purchased with grant in aid
from the V&A, London, The
Art Fund and The Friends of
the Potteries Museum & Art
Gallery, Stoke-on-Trent

Quart jug with Lady Godiva
and Peeping Tom, mid-
nineteenth century
Earthenware, transfer-printed
11.4 × 11.9 cm
Collection of the Herbert Art
Gallery & Museum, Coventry

Pablo Picasso
Female nude at the beach,
20 August 1963
Madoura pottery, France,
edition of 100
26 cm
Entrusted to the City
of Leicester by Sheila
and Richard Attenborough
to commemorate the lives
of their daughter Jane Mary
and granddaughter Lucy
Elizabeth who perished
together in the Asian tsunami
on 26 December 2004

Peter Blake
Babe Rainbow, 1967
Screenprint on tin,
edition of 10, 000
66 × 44.1 cm
University of Warwick
Art Collection

Jann Haworth
*Donuts, Coffee Cups and
Comics*, 1962
Cotton, thread, kapok, wood
65 × 36 × 54 cm
Wolverhampton Art Gallery
& Museums
Purchased for Wolverhampton
Art Gallery with assistance
from the MLA/V&A Purchase
Grant Fund and the Friends of
Wolverhampton Art Galleries

May Stevens
*Ordinary/Extraordinary (Rosa
Luxemburg)*, 1977
Screenprint on paper
45 × 60 cm
Wolverhampton Art Gallery
& Museums

Richard Hamilton
My Marilyn, 1966
Screenprint on paper,
edition of 75
70.7 × 80.9 cm
University of Warwick Art
Collection

Trade and Taste

Teapot and cover with
Chinoiserie figures, c.1775,
Staffordshire soft-paste
porcelain
13 x 9 x 11 cm
The Potteries Museum & Art
Gallery, Stoke-on-Trent

Teapot and cover with 'tree-
fence-house-tree' pattern,
c.1800
Staffordshire
Earthenware
12 × 9 × 11 cm
The Potteries Museum & Art
Gallery, Stoke-on-Trent

Teapot, c.1770–1780
Staffordshire
Earthenware
11.5 × 20.5 × 12.5 cm
Leicester Arts and
Museums Service

Brush pot, c.1800
Porcelain with blue
and white decoration
16.1 × 18 cm
Leicester Arts and
Museums Service

Large mug with an oriental
scene, c.1800
Earthenware with blue
and white decoration
16 × 16.5 × 11 cm
Nottingham City Museums
& Galleries

Vase, 1260–1400
Cizhou ware, Yuan Dynasty
Earthenware
20.5 × 15 cm
Collection of the Herbert Art
Gallery & Museum, Coventry

Small jug in Chinese style,
c.1770–1803
Lowestoft soft-paste porcelain
8.5 × 6 cm
Leamington Spa Art
Gallery & Museum
(Warwick District Council)

The Human Form

Pablo Picasso
Face, 17 January 1965
Madoura Pottery, France,
edition of 100
42.5 cm
Entrusted to the City of
Leicester by Sheila and
Richard Attenborough to
commemorate the lives of
their daughter Jane Mary
and granddaughter Lucy
Elizabeth who perished
together in the Asian tsunami
on 26th December 2004

Pablo Picasso
Face
17 January 1965, Madoura
Pottery, France,
edition of 100
42.5 cm
Entrusted to the City
of Leicester by Sheila
and Richard Attenborough
to commemorate the lives
of their daughter Jane Mary
and granddaughter Lucy
Elizabeth who perished
together in the Asian tsunami
on 26th December 2004

Vessel in the form of a man's
head, 400–600 AD
Peruvian (Mochican people)
Clay
19.5 × 16 × 14 cm
New Art Gallery Walsall

Mesopotamian figure,
c.3,000–2,500 BC
Clay
9.8 × 5.5 × 4.8 cm
New Art Gallery Walsall

Hans Coper
Large composite form, 1958–59
Earthenware
27 × 19 × 19 cm
Nottingham City Museums
& Galleries

Lucie Rie & Jean Ballantyne
Jean Ballantyne Memorial
Pot, 1985
Stoneware
36 × 15 × 12 cm
Nottingham City Museums
& Galleries

Face jug, 13th century,
Staffordshire
Earthenware
44.8 × 18.4 cm
Collection of the Herbert Art
Gallery & Museum, Coventry

R.B. Kitaj
Glue Words, 1968
Screenprint on paper,
edition of 70
85 × 59.6 cm
University of Warwick
Art Collection

R.B. Kitaj
Republic of the Southern Cross,
1965
Screenprint on paper,
edition of 70
63.5 × 102.5 cm
Rugby Art Gallery & Museum

Bob and Roberta Smith
*If you make art what happens
when you die?*, 2011
Installation comprising
67 parts
35.5 × 59.5 × 0.6 cm
New Art Gallery Walsall

Richard Hamilton
*Just what is it that makes
today's homes so different?*,
1992
Digital print on paper,
edition of 5,000
17 × 26.7 cm
Rugby Art Gallery & Museum

Grayson Perry
Designer Rebellion, 1999
Earthenware
85.8 × 33 × 33cm
The Potteries Museum &
Art Gallery, Stoke-on-Trent
Purchased through the
Contemporary Art Society
Special Collection Scheme
with Lottery funding from
Arts Council England, 2000

Eduardo Paolozzi
*Variations on a Geometric
Theme*, 1970
Wedgwood, Staffordshire,
edition of 200
Bone china with silk-
screenprint lithograph
26.8 cm
Courtesy of the Wedgwood
Museum Trust, Barlaston

Display 4

Twixt Two Worlds

Curatorial Fellow:
Gaia Tedone

Host venue:
Royal Pavilion &
Museums, Brighton
and Hove

Tour venue:
Towner, Eastbourne
10 October 2014 –
5 January 2015

Mary Burchett
Spirit Photograph, 1880s
Photographic print mounted
on Gold Edged card. Written
on Obverse.
17 × 10 cm
Donated anonymously to
Royal Pavilion & Museums,
Brighton & Hove

Mary Burchett
Spirit Photograph, c.1886
Photographic print mounted
on Gold Edged card. Written
on reverse.
16 × 11 cm
Donated anonymously to
Royal Pavilion & Museums,
Brighton & Hove

Mary Burchett
Spirit Photograph, c.1900
Photographic Print mounted
on card. Written on reverse.
14 × 11 cm
Donated anonymously to
Royal Pavilion & Museums,
Brighton & Hove

Mary Burchett
Spirit Photograph, c. 1886
Photographic print mounted
on Gold Edged card. Written
on reverse.
16 × 10 cm
Donated anonymously to
Royal Pavilion & Museums,
Brighton & Hove

Alfred Darling
*Alfred Darling Experimental
Cameras,* c. 1900
4 photographic prints on paper
Barnes Collection, Royal
Pavilion Museums, Brighton
& Hove

William Eglinton
Spirit Photograph, c. 1910
Photographic Print mounted
on card. Written on reverse.
14 × 11 cm
Donated anonymously to
Royal Pavilion & Museums,
Brighton & Hove

William Eglinton
Spirit Photograph, 1886
Photographic print mounted
on Gold Edged card. Written
on reverse.
16 × 10 cm
Donated anonymously to
Royal Pavilion & Museums,
Brighton & Hove

William Friese-Greene
Kino The Girl in Colour, 1920
Digital reconstruction of
original film reel
Bristol Record Office
Film Archive

Susan Hiller
The Fight, 2007
Photo-etching and aquatint on
copperplate with Hahnemühle
Etching paper
42 × 29.7 cm
Edition of 25
Commissioned by Matt's
Gallery for E3 4RR Print
Portfolio
Matt's Gallery, London

Albert Londe
*Three photos in a series showing
a hysterical woman yawning,*
c. 1890
Reproduction from the book
*Nouvelle Iconographie de la
Salpêtrière,* 1890
Wellcome Library, London

Albert Londe
*Suggestions par les sens dans la
periode cataleptique du grand
hypnotisme,* 1891
Reproduction from the book
*Nouvelle Iconographie de la
Salpêtrière,* 1890
Wellcome Library, London

Albert Londe
*Retraction nevropathique de
la paupiere superieure,* 1890
Reproduction from the book
*Nouvelle Iconographie de la
Salpêtrière,* 1890
Wellcome Library, London

Lumiere Brothers Production
Substitutions, 1896
Digitised version
Film Courtesy of the Trustees
of the Imperial War Museum

Thomas Hamilton McAllister
The sculptor's dream, c. 1870
Set of 5 dissolving views magic
lantern slides
18 × 10 cm
National Cinema Museum
Collection, Turin

Étienne Jules Marey
7 photographic magic lantern
slides, late 19th century
11 × 9 cm
Kingston Museum
& Heritage Service

Eadweard Muybridge
Palo Alto, California, 1881
13 x photographic magic
lantern slides
11 × 8.5 cm
Kingston Museum
& Heritage Service

Eadweard Muybridge
*An Electro-photographic
Investigation of consecutive
phases of animal movements.
Plate 349, Fencing,* 1872-1885
Original plate
60 × 48 cm
Royal Pavilion Museums,
Brighton & Hove

Eadweard Muybridge
*An Electro-photographic
investigation of consecutive
phases of animal movements,
Plate 60,* 1872 - 1886
Original plate
60 × 48 cm
Royal Pavilion Museums,
Brighton & Hove

Eadweard Muybridge
*An Electro-photographic
investigation of consecutive
phases of animal movements,
Plate 501,* 1872 - 1886
Original plate
60 × 48 cm
Royal Pavilion Museums,
Brighton & Hove

Eadweard Muybridge
An Electro-photographic investigation of consecutive phases of animal movements, plate 643, "Pandora" jumping a hurdle, bareback, clearing and landing; rider nude.
1872 - 1888
Original plate
60 × 48 cm
Royal Pavilion Museums, Brighton & Hove

Eadweard Muybridge
An Electro-photographic investigation of consecutive phases of animal movements,
1872 – 1889
Original plate
60 × 48 cm
Royal Pavilion Museums, Brighton & Hove

Saskia Olde Wolbers
Trailer, 2005
Single channel video
Projection
10 min
South London Gallery; purchased through the Contemporary Art Society Special Collection Scheme with Lottery funding from Arts Council England, 2005. London Borough of Southwark on behalf of the South London Gallery

R.W. Paul
Kruger's Dream of Empire, 1900
Digitised version
Film Courtesy of the Trustees of the Imperial War Museum

R.W. Paul
The '?' Motorist, 1906
Black and white, silent film.
2.22 min
BFI National Archive

Steven Pippin
Walking Naked, 1997
12 black and white photographs
86 × 86 cm
Swindon Museum and Art Gallery

John Arthur Roebuck Rudge
Portrait of William Friese-Greene, date unknown
2 photographs
16 × 12 cm, 7 × 7 cm
National Media Museum, Bradford

John Arthur Roebuck Rudge
2 prints from copy negatives of glass positive replica of Rudge's phantascope image, date unknown
photographic prints
22 × 17 cm
National Media Museum, Bradford

Two Clowns, 1906
Dir. George Albert Smith
Digital restoration and Kinemacolor re-creation
Nicholas Clark
Screen Archive South East, 2011

George Albert Smith
The X-Ray Fiend, 1897
Black and white silent film
0.44 min
BFI National Archive

George Albert Smith
Santa Claus, 1898
Black and white silent film
1.20 min
BFI National Archive

George Albert Smith
Mary Jane's Mishap, 1903
Black and white silent film
4.06 min
BFI National Archive

George Albert Smith
Santa Claus Film Frames, 1898
Black and White copy print of 9 consecutive frames from the film 'Santa Claus', 1898
Barnes Collection, Royal Pavilion Museums, Brighton & Hove

William Fox Talbot
The Latticed Window
Photograph on paper (2009 digitised copy from the original negative which dates from 1835)
31 × 25 cm
National Media Museum, Bradford

William Fox Talbot
Three Sculptural Objects, date unknown
Photograph on paper
15 × 15 cm
The British Library

William Fox Talbot
Three Graces (print),
c. 1840-1849
Photographic print on paper
15 × 13 cm
The British Library

William Fox Talbot
Three Graces (negative), date unknown
Calotype negative
14 × 13 cm
The British Library

The Artist's Nightmare
26 September 1908,
Warwick Trading Company
Screen Archive South East

James Williamson
A Big Swallow, 1901
Black and white silent film
1.08 min
BFI National Archive

James Williamson
The Little Match Seller, 1902
3.15 min
BFI National Archive

Magic Lanterns, Slides and Cameras

Biunial Lantern, c. 1850
Mahogany body and slide stages with lacquer brass fitting
72 × 22 × 47.5 cm
Royal Pavilion Museums, Brighton & Hove

Alfred Darling & Sons Ltd.
The Biokam, 1889
Variable dimensions
Barnes Collection, Royal Pavilion Museums, Brighton & Hove

Alfred Darling & Sons
Darling 'Special Effects' Cine-Camera, 1899-1900
Mahogany
30.6 × 23.5 × 32.5 cm
Barnes Collection, Royal Pavilion Museums, Brighton & Hove

T. & H. Doublet
Improved Phantasmagoria and Dissolving View Lanterns, 1860
76 × 21 × 40.5 cm
National Museum of Cinema, Turin

John Arthur Roebuck Rudge
Replica of Rudge Fantascope Lantern produced by the Science Museum, London
Lantern and set of slides
National Media Museum, Bradford

Group of 8 magic lantern slides, c.1900
Magic lantern slides
8 × 8 cm each
Royal Pavilion Museums, Brighton & Hove

Lighthouse, c. 1850's
3 wooden frame magic lantern slides painted on glass
18 × 10 cm each
Bristol Museum and Art Gallery

The Tower of London (day and night), c. 1850's
2 wooden frame magic lantern slides painted on glass
18 × 10 cm
Bristol Museum and Art Gallery

Magician's Cauldron,
Set of 2 dissolving view magic lantern slides, paint on glass
18 × 10 cm
National Cinema Museum Collection, Turin

The Soldier's Dream, late 19th century
Set of 6 dissolving view magic lantern slides, paint on glass
18 × 10 cm
National Cinema Museum Collection, Turin

Train Leaving the Station, late 19th century
Animated magic lantern slides
18 × 10 cm
National Cinema Museum Collection, Turin

Ephemera

Ray Allister
*Friese-Greene Close-up
of an Inventor,* c. 1951
Book
22 × 15 cm
Barnes Collection, Royal
Pavilion Museums, Brighton
& Hove

William Friese-Greene
*Invitation to the Barnes Brothers
for the evening 'who invented
cinema?' 26th October 1995,
reception followed at MoMi.*
From *The Magic Box* 1954 film.
Postcard invite
Barnes Collection, Royal
Pavilion Museums, Brighton
& Hove

W.C. Hughes
The Art of Projection, 1897
Book
21.4 × 14.3 × 2 cm
Barnes Collection, Royal
Pavilion Museums, Brighton
& Hove

Georges Sadoul
*British Creators of Film
Technique,* 1948
Booklet
21 × 14 cm
Barnes Collection, Royal
Pavilion Museums, Brighton
& Hove

George Albert Smith
The Corsican Brothers, 1898
Postcard
13 × 8 cm
Barnes Collection, Royal
Pavilion Museums, Brighton
& Hove

George Albert Smith
In the Tunnel, from George
Albert Smith's 1899 film
Colour and black & white
photographic postcards
13 × 9 cm
Barnes Collection, Royal
Pavilion Museums, Brighton
& Hove

Picture Post Magazine
1949
Magazine
33 × 25 cm
National Media Museum,
Bradford

St. Ann's Wells Garden, Hove,
early 20th century
Postcard
Barnes Collection, Royal
Pavilion Museums, Brighton
& Hove

St. Ann's Wells Garden, Hove,
early 20th century
Photograph on paper
16 × 24 cm
Barnes Collection, Royal
Pavilion Museums, Brighton
& Hove

St. Ann's Wells Garden, Hove,
early 20th century
Illustration
19 × 24 cm
Barnes Collection, Royal
Pavilion Museums, Brighton
& Hove

St. Ann's Wells Garden, Hove,
early 20th century
Card; Cellulose acetate
8 × 13 cm
Barnes Collection, Royal
Pavilion Museums, Brighton
& Hove

Brighton Aquarium, early
20th century
Postcard
13 × 9 cm
Barnes Collection, Royal
Pavilion Museums, Brighton
& Hove

Brighton Aquarium, early
20th century
Postcard
14 × 9 cm
Barnes Collection, Royal
Pavilion Museums, Brighton
& Hove

William Friese-Greene Portrait
Photograph
Barnes Collection, Royal
Pavilion Museums, Brighton
& Hove

*George Albert Smith at his desk
with film measurer and Urban
Bioscope*
Photograph on paper
Barnes Collection, Royal
Pavilion Museums, Brighton
& Hove

*John Barnes in front of William
Friese-Greene plaque in Bristol*
Photograph on paper
Barnes Collection, Royal
Pavilion Museums, Brighton
& Hove

Alhambra Theatre, 1907
Programme
Barnes Collection, Royal
Pavilion Museums, Brighton
& Hove

Bioscope Animated Pictures,
early 20th century
Photograph
Barnes Collection, Royal
Pavilion Museums, Brighton
& Hove

*Brighton Aquarium Programme,
George Albert Smith,* early 20th
century
Paper
Barnes Collection, Royal
Pavilion Museums, Brighton
& Hove

*Black and white print of Wrench
Cinematograph,* early 20th
century
Black and White print
(illustration) on photographic
paper
9 × 9 cm
Barnes Collection, Royal
Pavilion Museums, Brighton
& Hove

Charles Urban Studio, early
20th century
Photograph
25 × 20 cm
Barnes Collection, Royal
Pavilion Museums, Brighton
& Hove

*Warwick Trading Company
studio,* early 20th century
Photograph on paper
Barnes Collection, Royal
Pavilion Museums, Brighton
& Hove

Please note the List of Works
refers to the Whitechapel Gallery
displays, additional works were
included in the touring exhibitions.

Lenders

Abbot Hall Art Gallery, Lakeland Arts Trust

British Council Film Collection

British Film Institute

Bolton Library and Museum Services

Bristol Museums, Galleries & Archives

Bristol Record Office Film Archive

British Library

Cambridge University Library

The Collection and Usher Gallery, Lincoln

Ferens Art Gallery

Gainsborough Old Hall

Grundy Art Gallery

Harris Museum & Art Gallery

Hatton Gallery, Newcastle University

Herbert Art Gallery & Museum

Imperial War Museum

Kirklees Collection, Huddersfield Art Gallery

Laing Art Gallery, Tyne & Wear Museums

Lancashire Archives

Leamington Spa Art Gallery & Museum

Leeds Museums and Galleries (Leeds Art Gallery)

Leicester Arts & Museums Service

Manchester City Galleries

Manchester Libraries, Information and Archives, Manchester City Council

Matt's Gallery, London

Museum of Lincolnshire Life

Muybridge Collection, Kingston Museum Collections

National Media Museum Bradford

National Cinema Museum Collection, Turin

New Art Gallery Walsall

Norwich Castle Museum & Art Gallery

Nottingham City Museums & Galleries

The Potteries Museum & Art Gallery

Royal Pavilion & Museums, Brighton & Hove

Rugby Art Gallery & Museum

Peter Scott Gallery, Lancaster University

Screen Archive South East

South London Gallery

South Shields Museum & Art Gallery

Swindon Museum & Art Gallery

The Tennyson Research Centre

University of Bristol Theatre Collection

University of Warwick Art Collection

The Wedgwood Museum Trust

Wellcome Library, London

Whitworth Art Gallery, University of Manchester

Williamson Art Gallery & Museum

Wolverhampton Art Gallery & Museums

York Museums Trust (York Art Gallery)

Contemporary Art Society
1910-2014

1910

Founded

The Contemporary Art Society is founded by Charles Aitken, Director of Whitechapel Art Gallery; Roger Fry, Curator of Metropolitan Museum of Modern Art, New York; Charles J. Holmes, Director of the National Portrait Gallery; Ernest Marsh, expert in Martinware pottery; D.S. MacColl, Keeper of the Tate Gallery; Philip Morrell, a Liberal MP; Lady Ottoline Morrell, patron of the arts. The first meeting is held in Lady Ottoline Morrell's drawing room in Bedford Square, London in April.

Purchase

Augustus John, *Smiling Woman* (1908–09), oil on canvas, is the Contemporary Art Society's first purchase and is presented to the Tate Gallery in 1917. The first of his works to enter a UK public collection.

1911

Gift

Gwen John, *Nude Girl* (1909–10), oil on canvas, is gifted to the Contemporary Art Society by a member of the committee and presented to the Tate Gallery in 1917.

Purchase

Eric Gill, *Crucifixion* (1910), hoptonwood stone relief, is purchased by Roger Fry and Robert Ross and presented to the Tate Gallery in 1920.

1912

Committee

First annual report published. Purchases are made by one member of the committee appointed to buy for six months. One hundred and forty-one private subscribers are listed as members paying one guinea each.

Museums

First public collections join as members: Ulster Museum, National Museums Northern Ireland, Belfast, New Walk Museum & Art Gallery, Leicester and Manchester Art Gallery.

1913

Exhibition

First public exhibition in London of the works acquired by the society by both gift and purchase held at The Goupil Gallery 1–12 April, including works by 82 artists including Vanessa Bell, Jacob Epstein, Augustus John, Wyndham Lewis and Ethel Sands.

1914

Purchase

Sir Jacob Epstein, *Euphemia Lamb* (1908), bronze is purchased by the committee and presented to the Tate Gallery in 1917.

Purchase

Walter Sickert, *Ennui* (c.1914), oil on canvas, is purchased and presented to the Tate Gallery in 1924.

Augustus John, *Woman Smiling*, 1908–09. Presented by the Contemporary Art Society 1917 © Tate, London 2014

1916

Gift

C.R.W. Nevinson, *La Mitraillleuse* (1915), oil on canvas, is gifted anonymously to the Contemporary Art Society and presented to the Tate Gallery in 1917.

1917

Gift

Paul Gauguin, *Tahitians* (c.1891), oil, crayon and charcoal on paper, is gifted to the Contemporary Art Society by Roger Fry. It is presented to the Tate Gallery in 1917, one of the first works by a non-British artist to be gifted by the Contemporary Art Society.

1919

Purchasing Scheme

The prints and drawings fund is founded, led by Campbell Dodgson, Keeper of Prints and Drawings at the British Museum. The purchased works are shown throughout the country before they are presented to the British Museum, including works by Edgar Degas, Henri de Toulouse-Lautrec and Jean Marchand. The fund has a separate subscription fee.

1921

Purchase

Stanley Spencer, *Christ Carrying the Cross* (1920), oil on canvas, is purchased by Muirhead Bone and presented to the Tate Gallery in 1925.

1923

Exhibition

Exhibition at Grosvenor House.

Purchase

Vanessa Bell, *Chrysanthemums* (1920), oil on canvas, is purchased by Sir Edward Marsh and presented to the Tate Gallery in 1924. It is the first of her works to enter the Tate collection.

1924

Exhibition

The British Museum holds an exhibition of prints and drawings presented by the Contemporary Art Society. There are further exhibitions in 1936 and 1940.

1925

The length of time given to committee members for purchases increases to twelve months.

Gift

Sydney Schiff gifts 42 works to the Contemporary Art Society. Predominantly works on paper, the gift included 13 works by Wyndham Lewis as well as David Bomberg, Frank Dobson and John Currie. He also donates 2 works by Henri Gaudier-Brzeska and Ossip Zadkine to the newly-created Foreign Fund, set up in the same year, which purchases and gifts works by contemporary artists born outside Great Britain.

1928

Purchasing Scheme

The Pottery and Craft Fund is set up, led by Ernest Marsh (the fund ran until 1948). Early purchases included works by William Staite Murray, Charles Vyse, Bernard Leach, Shoji Hamada and a goose by Barbara Skeaping, potentially the first work by Barbara Hepworth acquired by the Contemporary Art Society. In its first distribution ten works were presented to the V&A, five to University College Wales, seven to the Hanley, Stoke-on-Trent, eleven to the City and County Museum, Bristol, and nine to the Leicester Museum.

1929

Purchase

The Lloyd Patterson Fund buys 20 works for the Ulster Museum, National Museums Northern Ireland, Belfast.

1930

Gift

C. Frank Stoop gifts three sculptures and 17 drawings by Henri Gaudier-Brzeska to the Tate Gallery through the Contemporary Art Society. These included *Red Stone Dancer* (1913), *Singer* (1913) and *The Imp* (c.1914). Stoop was to bequeath the rest of his collection to the Tate Gallery in 1933.

Chairman

Sir Cyril Kendall Butler becomes Chairman (until 1936).

Purchase

Seventeen drawings and 176 prints purchased through the Print Fund are presented to the British Museum. An additional 49 works are then presented in 1931.

1931

Charity

Contemporary Art Society becomes a registered charity.

Gift

Ben Nicholson, *St Ives Bay: sea with boats* (1931), oil and pencil on canvas, is gifted to the Contemporary Art Society by Lord Henry Bentick and presented to Manchester City Galleries in 1950.

Trip

Private collection visits this year include Mr. and Mrs. Courtauld – Samuel Courtauld was both a committee member and purchaser – and Blenheim Palace.

1932

Staff

Maynard Keynes joins the committee and takes charge of the Foreign Fund in 1934.

1933

Purchase

Pablo Picasso, *Flowers* (1901), oil on canvas, gifted to the Tate Gallery, it was the first work by Pablo Picasso to be bought by Tate. The Contemporary Art Society later gifted a second work by Picasso – *The Dove* (1952), lithograph – to the Grundy Art Gallery, Blackpool in 1977.

1936

Chairman

Sir Edward Marsh becomes Chairman (until 1952).

1939

Purchase

First work by Henry Moore is purchased by Sir Kenneth Clark. *Recumbent Figure* (1938), green hornton stone, is presented to the Tate Gallery the same year.

Contemporary
Art Society
Annual Report
(cover),
1940–41 ©
Contemporary
Art Society

Pablo Picasso,
Flowers, 1901.
Purchased
with assistance
from the
Contemporary
Art Society
1933 ©
Succession
Picasso/DACS,
London 2014.
Photo: © Tate,
London 2014

1940

Purchase

Stanley Spencer, *The Nursery* (1936), oil on canvas, is presented to the Museum of Modern Art, New York.

Committee

Sir Kenneth Clark joins the committee.

1941

Museums

Museum membership expands to include the Commonwealth, with members from Canada, Australia, New Zealand and South Africa.

1944

Purchase

Paul Nash, *Landscape of the Moon's Last Phase* (1943–44), oil on canvas, is presented to Walker Art Gallery, Liverpool.

Staff

Denis Mathews becomes Assistant Secretary, initiating the Contemporary Art Society exhibitions at the Tate Gallery as well as social occasions such as private collection visits and private views.

Purchase

The Contemporary Art Society presents four works to the National Gallery of New South Wales, having begun its membership in 1941. These were Stanley Spencer, *The Scrap Heap* (1944), Augustus John, *Welsh Mountains in Snow* (c.1911), Paul Nash, *Sunflower and Sun* (1942) and Frances Hodgkins, *Courtyard, Corfe Castle* (1942). Later works presented to the gallery include works on paper by Henry Moore and Henri Matisse, and sculptures by Alison Wilding and Lilliane Lijn.

1945

Purchasing Scheme

Lady Sempil takes over the Pottery and Crafts Fund after the death of Ernest Marsh.

1946

Purchase

The first work by Francis Bacon is purchased, *Study for the Magdalene – Figure Study II* (1946), oil on canvas, is presented to Batley Art Gallery, now Huddersfield Art Gallery, Kirklees Museums and Galleries, in 1952. The Contemporary Art Society has gifted a total of five works by Francis Bacon to museum members.

1947

Patron

Her Majesty Queen Elizabeth The Queen Mother becomes Royal Patron until her death in March 2002.

Gift

Sir Kenneth Clark gifts the first of 68 works to the Contemporary Art Society between 1947 and 1951.

1948

Publication

From Sickert to 1948 is published by Lund Humphries, the first history of the Contemporary Art Society through the works purchased and gifted to museum members.

1950

Purchase

Lucian Freud, *Still Life with Squid and Sea Urchin* (1949), oil on copper, is purchased by Robin Ironside and presented to the Harris Museum and Art Gallery, Preston in 1952.

1951

Purchase

Ben Nicholson, *Still Life with Guitar* (1933), oil on canvas, is presented to Leeds Art Gallery.

Purchase

Peter Lanyon, *Porthleven* (1951), oil on board, is purchased by Sir Philip Hendry and presented to the Tate Gallery in 1953.

C·A·S
1953 Membership Card

1953

Bequest

Sir Edward Marsh bequeaths his collection of nearly 200 paintings, drawings and sculptures to the Contemporary Art Society, which is then distributed to 80 member museums and galleries, including work by Stanley Spencer, Duncan Grant, Mark Gertler, Paul Nash and Vanessa Bell.

Publication

Publication about Sir Edward Marsh, *Eddie Marsh* is co-published by the Contemporary Art Society and Lund Humphries.

Membership

Membership of the Contemporary Art Society reaches 1,750, having been 300 in 1946.

Exhibition

The Contemporary Art Society holds its first exhibition at the Tate Gallery, 'Figures in their Settings', which includes new work by Barbara Hepworth, Patrick Heron, William Scott and Lynn Chadwick.

1954   **Purchasing Scheme**

The Prints and Drawings Fund merges with the general purchasing scheme.

1955   **Purchase**

Victor Pasmore, *Motif in Indian Red and Mustard* (c.1950), oil on canvas on board, is purchased by Howard Bliss and presented to National Museums Liverpool in 1956.

1956   **Director**

Pauline Vogelpoel becomes Organising Secretary (she was then Director from 1976 until departing in 1982).

Chairman

Sir Colin Anderson becomes Chairman (until 1960).

Exhibition

'The Seasons' is held at the Tate Gallery, with new work by 57 artists, including Patrick Heron, Terry Frost, William Scott, Humphrey Spender, Robert Adam, Kenneth Armitage, Lynn Chadwick, Elisabeth Frink, Barbara Hepworth and Robert Clatworthy. The Contemporary Art Society purchases some of the works, which are then distributed to museum members, including Patrick Heron, *Winter Harbour* (1955–56), presented to Vancouver Art Gallery in 1959, and Reg Butler, *Torso* (1956), presented to Manchester City Galleries in 1959.

1958   **Exhibition**

The Contemporary Art Society exhibition 'The Religious Theme' with works by 80 artists is held at the Tate Gallery.

Purchase

Elisabeth Frink, *Wild Boar* (1958) is purchased by Anthony Lousada and presented to the National Gallery of Queensland, Brisbane in 1960.

1959   **Purchase**

Peter Blake, *On the Balcony* (1955–57), oil on canvas, is purchased by Bryan Robertson and presented to the Tate Gallery in 1963.

Collections
in Palace Gate, Kensington, W.8.

Contemporary Art Society
Card of Admission for

1 Captain Ernest Duveen, 8 Palace Gate
2 Mr and Mrs H. P. Juda, The Penthouse, 10 Palace Gate
3 Mr and Mrs Grahame Davies, Flat 17, 10 Palace Gate
4 Mr and Mrs David Breeden, Flat 14a, 10 Palace Gate
5 Mr and Mrs Peter Adam, Flat 12, 10 Palace Gate

Please view these collections in the above order presenting this card at Captain Duveen's flat at

on Saturday, March 15.

Notice
Members are asked to arrive punctually and to limit their visits as far as possible in order to accomodate those following them at given times

Buses: Nos: 9, 73, 52, 49
Underground: Kensington High Street, Gloucester Road

Ephemera detailing five public collection visits, 1958 © Contemporary Art Society c/o Tate Archive

'The First Fifty Years', installation photograph at Tate, 1960 © Contemporary Art Society c/o Tate Archive. Photo: Gerald Howson

'British Painting in the Sixties', installation photograph at the Whitechapel Gallery, 1963 © Contemporary Art Society c/o Tate Archive. Photo: Graham Kirk

1960

Exhibition

Fiftieth-anniversary exhibition at the Tate Gallery. 'The First Fifty Years' is a display of 2,000 works that had been gifted to museums and galleries in Britain and the Commonwealth including works by Francis Bacon, Augustus John and Walter Sickert.

Chairman

Sir Whitney Straight becomes Chairman (until 1971).

1961

Trip

The first Contemporary Art Society Members' trip abroad to Amsterdam.

1962

Trip

Twenty-one day trip for members to New York and Mexico.

Purchase

Karel Appel, *Têtes over de Landscape* (1959), gouache, is purchased by Lord Croft and presented to Sheffield Galleries & Museums Trust, Graves Art Gallery in 1965.

1963

Exhibition

The Contemporary Art Society exhibition 'British Painting in the Sixties', held at the Tate Gallery and the Whitechapel Gallery. The Contemporary Art Society purchased several works from the exhibition including Frank Auerbach, *Maples Demolition, Euston Road* (1960), oil on board, presented to Leeds Art Gallery in 1964, and Howard Hodgkin, *Staff Meeting* (1960), oil on canvas, presented to Kettering Art Gallery in 1964. The exhibition had over 40,000 visitors and was the first of the Contemporary Art Society exhibitions to tour abroad.

1964

Purchase

Takis, *Electro Signals, No 1* (date unknown) is purchased by Sir John Rothenstein and presented to Birmingham City Art Gallery in 1968, one of the only kinetic works to be acquired.

Trip

Members and patrons trip to Hong Kong and Tokyo.

Pauline Vogelpoel (third from left) and the Contemporary Art Society members at Hong Kong airport, 1964 © Contemporary Art Society c/o Tate Archive. Photo: Cathay Pacific Airways Ltd., Hong Kong

1965

Exhibition

The Contemporary Art Society exhibition 'British Sculpture in the Sixties', held at the Tate Gallery and the Whitechapel Gallery, with 12 younger sculptors invited to take part in a 'New Generation' section at the Whitechapel Gallery. Among the purchases made by the Contemporary Art Society are Anthony Caro, *Early One Morning* (1962) painted steel, presented to the Tate Gallery in 1965, and Robert Adams, *Circular Form and Bar* (1962), bronzed steel.

Grant

The Contemporary Art Society provides a grant to the Tate Gallery to support the purchase of *The Three Dancers* (1925), oil on canvas, by Pablo Picasso.

Trip

Twenty-day members' trip to New York, Cleveland, Los Angeles, Santa Barbara, San Francisco, Chicago and Washington.

1967

Purchase

Henry Moore, *Knife Edge – Two Piece* (1967), bronze, is presented to the City of Westminster by the Contemporary Art Society and the artist.

1969

Purchase

Ian Hamilton-Finlay, *Drift* (1968), wood, is purchased by David Thompson and presented to Towner, Eastbourne, in 1971.

Trip

Members and patrons' trip to Pakistan, Afghanistan, Kashmir and Nepal as well as visits to the studios of Eileen Agar, Patrick Caulfield, Howard Hodgkin, F.E. McWilliam and Bridget Riley.

1970

Performance

Peter Logan's *Mechanical Ballet*, is produced with assistance from the Contemporary Art Society and previews at the Gulbenkian Hall, Royal College of Art, on 5 May.

1971

Chairman

Peter Meyer becomes Chairman (until 1976).

Purchase

John Latham, *P – (N) 2:5/12* (1962), acrylic on canvas, is purchased by Nancy Balfour and is presented to Whitworth Art Gallery in 1979.

'Works on
Paper: The
Contemporary
Art Society
gift to Public
Galleries
1952–1977',
poster, 1977 ©
Contemporary
Art Society

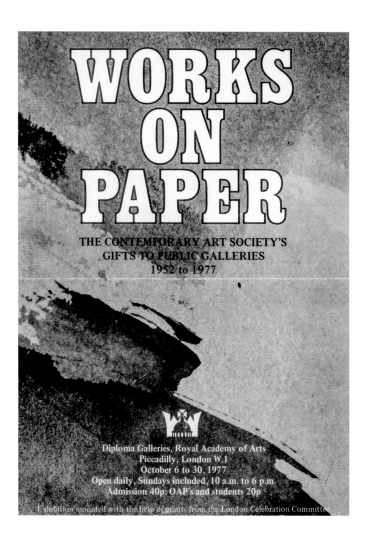

1973

Purchase

Richard Hamilton, *Five Tyres Remoulded*
(1972), nine screenprints on polyester,
is purchased by Alexander Dunbar and
presented to the Tate Gallery in 1975.

Purchase

John Hilliard, 12 & 10 *Representations
of Brighton Sea Front* (date unknown),
two units with colour negatives,
is purchased by Carol Hogden and
presented to the V&A Circulation
Department in 1975.

1974

Funding

The Contemporary Art Society receives
first Arts Council funding with a £2,000
grant towards acquisitions, which increases
to £5,000 by 1976.

Purchase

Bruce Nauman, *War* (1971), screenprint,
and *Green* (1971) screenprint, are purchased
by Max Gordon and presented to
museums in New Zealand in 1975
and 1979 respectively.

Gift

Two Derek Jarman paintings are gifted
anonymously to the Contemporary Art
Society: *Avebury Series 2* (1973), acrylic
on canvas, is presented to Derby Museum
and Art Gallery, and *Avebury Series 4*
(1973), acrylic on canvas, is presented
to Northampton Art Gallery, both in
1974. Two further Derek Jarman works
are purchased with an anonymous
donation: *Shad Thames Series 2* (date
unknown), acrylic on canvas, and *Shad
Thames Series 4* (date unknown), acrylic
on canvas, in the same year.

1975

Fair

The Contemporary Art Society organises
Art Fair at the Mall Galleries.

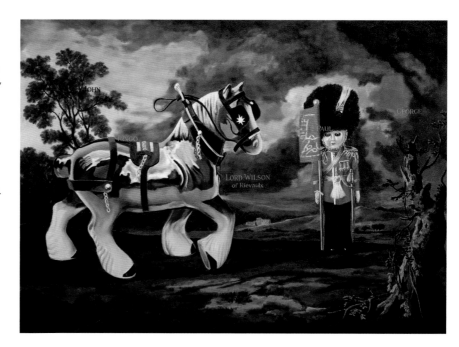

Mark Wallinger, *Lost Horizons* (1986), oil on canvas, 152 x 214 cm. Collection of The Potteries Museum and Art Gallery, Stoke-on-Trent © the artist. Courtesy the artist and Hauser & Wirth. Presented by the Contemporary Art Society, 1989

1976

Nancy Balfour OBE becomes Chairman (until 1982).

1977

Exhibition

The Contemporary Art Society exhibition 'American Art at Home in Britain: The Last Four Decades', paintings and sculpture by post-war American artists at the US Embassy. Organised in co-operation with the United States Information Service.

Funding

The Contemporary Art Society receives it's first funding from the Scottish Arts Council with a £1,000 grant to purchase work by Scottish artists to ensure they are better represented with UK public collections.

Purchase

Two of the buyers in 1977, Joanna Drew and Gabrielle Keillier, acquire the largest number of photographic works of any year thus far with purchases of work by Fay Godwin, John Harper, John Kirkwood and Glen Onwin. Marc Chaimowitz, *Dream* (1977), photomontage in three parts, is purchased by Joanna Drew and presented to Norwich City Museum and Art Gallery in 1979.

Corporate

First corporate contract with De Beers.

1981

Gift

Twenty-eight works by David Bomberg are gifted to seven UK public collections by Mr. and Mrs. J. Newark.

1982

Purchase

Lucie Rie, *Stoneware Bowl and Bottle* (1980) is presented to the National Museum of Wales, Cardiff.

Director

Petronilla Silver becomes Director (until 1993).

Chairman

Caryl Hubbard becomes Chairman (until 1990).

THE CONTEMPORARY ART SOCIETY

EIGHTY YEARS OF COLLECTING

1983 **Purchasing Scheme**

The Contemporary Art Society launches a new craft scheme after securing an annual grant of £4,000 from the Crafts Council. Thirty-one museums and galleries join the scheme in the first year, with Ann Sutton undertaking the first year of purchasing. In the same year, the Henry Moore Foundation starts providing an annual grant for the purchase of sculpture.

1984 **Fair**

The Contemporary Art Society Art Market, is staged for the first time, later to become ART*futures*.

Purchase

Gilbert and George, *Good* (1984), is purchased by Marina Vaizey and presented to Wolverhampton Art Gallery in 1986.

1985 **Anniversary**

Peter Blake designs a poster for the Contemporary Art Society's 75th birthday. It is later presented to Tate Gallery'.

1986 **Purchase**

Mark Wallinger, *Lost Horizons* (1986), oil on canvas, is purchased by Stephen Tumim and presented to The Potteries Museum & Art Gallery, Stoke-on-Trent in 1989.

1988 **Consultancy**

Contemporary Art Society Projects is created.

Purchase

Alison Wilding, *Hand to Mouth* (1986), lead, steel, brass and beeswax pigment, is purchased with support from the Henry Moore Foundation and presented to the Scottish National Gallery of Modern Art, Edinburgh in 1992.

1990 **Chairman**

David Gordon becomes Chairman (until 1998).

Public Programme

Nicholas Serota, Director of Tate, gives the Contemporary Art Society Annual Lecture at the Royal Society of Arts.

1991 **Purchasing Scheme**

A new purchasing model called the Pilot Collections Scheme is developed and tested with three member museums: Ferens Art Gallery, Hull, Wolverhampton Art Gallery and Towner, Eastbourne.

Publication

British Contemporary Art 1910-1990: Eighty Years of Collecting by the Contemporary Art Society is published by Herbert. It includes contributions by Alan Bowness, Richard Cork, Edward Lucie-Smith and Marina Vaizey.

Purchase

Richard Long, *Untitled* (1991), mud on paper, presented to the Tate Gallery in memory of Adrian Ward-Jackson.

Damien Hirst,
*Forms Without
Life*, 1991.
Presented
by the
Contemporary
Art Society,
1992. © Damien
Hirst and
Science Ltd.
All rights
reserved,
DACS 2014.
Photo: © Tate,
London 2014

Mona Hatoum,
*A Couple
(of swings)*,
1993, glass
plates,
stainless steel
and fixtures,
245 x 66 x 130
cm. Collection
of The Herbert
Art Gallery
and Museum,
Coventry ©
Mona Hatoum.
Courtesy
Galerie Chantal
Crousel.
Presented
by the
Contemporary
Art Society with
support of the
Henry Moore
Foundation,
2004

Trip

Twelve-day trip for members and patrons
to New Orleans, Charleston and Savannah.

Exhibition

'The Contemporary Art Society: Eighty
Years of Collecting' is held at the Hayward
Gallery. The exhibited works were selected
from over 5000 acquisitions by Joanna
Drew, Director of the Hayward Gallery
and Regional Exhibitions at the Southbank
Centre. It toured to the Maclaurin Art
Gallery, Ayr; Bristol City Museum and Art
Gallery and Walker Art Gallery, Liverpool
throughout 1992.

1992   **Purchase**

Damien Hirst, *Forms Without Life* (1991),
fibreboard cabinet, melamine, wood,
steel, glass and sea shells, is purchased
by Penelope Govett and presented to
the Tate Gallery. The first work by Hirst
to enter the Tate collection.

1993   **Director**

Gill Hedley becomes Director (until 2006).

1994   **Purchase**

Mona Hatoum, *A Couple (of swings)* (1993),
stainless steel and glass, is purchased with
support from the Henry Moore Foundation
by Edward Lee. It is presented to the
Herbert Art Gallery & Museum, Coventry
in 1996.

Purchase

Peter Doig, *Concrete Cabin* (1992), oil
on canvas, is purchased by Edward Lee
and presented to Leicester Museum
& Art Gallery in 1996.

1995   **Purchase**

Douglas Gordan, *Hysterical* (1995), video,
is purchased with support from the Henry
Moore Foundation by Richard Cork and
presented to Southampton City Art
Gallery in 1996.

Sarah Lucas, *Divine*, 1991 from *Self Portraits 1990-1998*, 1999, portfolio of twelve iris prints, 60 x 80 cm, edition of 150. Copyright the artist, courtesy Sadie Coles HQ, London. South London Gallery; purchased through the Contemporary Art Society Special Collection Scheme with Lottery funding from Arts Council England, 2000

Purchase

Gillian Wearing, *Signs that say what you want them to say and not signs that say what someone else wants you to say* (1992–93), six c-type prints, is purchased by Richard Cork and presented to Leamington Spa Art Gallery & Museum in 1996.

1996

Exhibition

Take it From Here', the exhibition of works to be distributed to museum members is held exclusively outside of London for the first time in three venues in Sunderland to coincide with the launch of the Year of Visual Arts UK in the Northern Arts region. The Contemporary Art Society is instrumental in bringing together three national institutions that purchase contemporary art – Arts Council England, the Tate Gallery and the Crafts Council – to highlight their contemporary acquisitions and the practice of contemporary collecting.

1997

Bequest

The Nancy Balfour Bequest of over 400 works is distributed to member museums, including work by Bridget Riley, Henry Moore, Eduardo Paolozzi, Lynn Chadwick, Patrick Heron, Victor Pasmore and Andy Goldsworthy.

Premises

The Contemporary Art Society leaves the offices at the Tate Gallery, moving to Bloomsbury.

1998

Chairman

Oliver Prenn becomes Chairman (until 2006).

Purchasing Scheme

Arts Council England awards the Contemporary Art Society a £2.5 million grant from National Lottery capital funds to establish the Special Collections Scheme, through which 610 works by 313 artists and makers were purchased for 18 collections across England in order to develop challenging collections of contemporary art in regional museums. This included work by Yinka Shonibare, Richard Wright, Tracey Emin, Damien Hirst, Grayson Perry, Jeremy Deller, Goshka Macuga, Tony Oursler, Gillian Wearing and Tomoko Takahashi and commissions by Bill Fontana, Christian Boltanski and William Furlong. The scheme ended in 2005.

CASt – Contemporary Art Society Tours – take place for the first time with Contemporary Art Society staff taking members to new galleries and artist-run spaces in London.

1999

Funding

The Esmée Fairbairn Charitable Trust awards the Contemporary Art Society £60,000 for a three-year project to enable six new museums to join as museum members whilst also enabling the Contemporary Art Society to develop an education programme that enhances gifts to museums.

Purchase

Grayson Perry, *Designer Rebellion* (1999, earthenware, and *Video Installation* (1999), earthenware, are presented to The Potteries Museum and Art Gallery, Stoke-on-Trent through the Special Collection Scheme.

2000

Purchase

Jeremy Deller, *I Love Melancholy* (2000), wall painting, matt emulsion and gloss paint, is presented to Southampton City Art Gallery through the Special Collection Scheme.

Purchase

Sarah Lucas, *Self Portraits 1990–1999* (1999), portfolio of 12 iris prints on fine art watercolour paper with signed and dated colophon page in card portfolio, is presented to South London Gallery through the Special Collection Scheme .

2003

Purchasing Scheme

National Collecting Scheme for Scotland is established. The scheme enabled contemporary artwork to be purchased for six museums and galleries in Scotland, including work by Jim Lambie, Martin Boyce, Claire Barclay, Graham Fagan and Julian Opie.

Gift

The John A. Walker archive collection of 1970s political paintings, prints, art texts and posters including works by Art & Language, Derek Boshier, Lawrence Weiner and Peter Kennard is gifted to Wolverhampton Art Gallery.

Olafur Eliasson, *The Forked Forest Path,* 1998, branches and saplings. Courtesy Towner Collection © 1998 Olafur Eliasson. Towner, Eastbourne; purchased through the Contemporary Art Society Special Collection Scheme with Lottery funding from Arts Council England, 2003

Purchase

Olafur Eliasson, *The Forked Forest Path* (1998), branches and saplings, is presented to Towner, Eastbourne through the Special Collection Scheme. The first of his works to enter a regional public collection in the UK. The work is included in the subsequent exhibition 'Landscape? New Definitions through the Contemporary Art Society Special Collection Scheme 1999–2003', which also includes works by Tania Kovats, Joachim Koester, Rut Blees Luxemburg and Ceal Floyer.

2004

Exhibition

'Tom Bendhem: Collector', an exhibition of the collection of long-standing patron bequeathed to the Contemporary Art Society opens and tours throughout 2005/6.

Purchase

Anya Gallacio, *While Reaching for Alma Ata* (2004) is presented to The Potteries Museum & Art Gallery, Stoke-on-Trent through the Special Collection Scheme.

2006

Chairman

Alison Myners becomes Chairman (until 2010).

Purchase

Five works by Wolfgang Tillmans, including *Tomatoes* (2003) and *Tree Filling Window* (2002), both c-type photographic prints, are presented to The McManus, Dundee's Art Gallery & Museum through the National Collecting Scheme for Scotland, and are the first to enter a public collection in Scotland.

2007

Bequest

Distribution of the Tom Bendhem Bequest, including work by Bruce McLean, David Mach, Georg Baselitz, Bridget Riley and Zadok Ben David.

Director

Paul Hobson becomes Director (until 2013).

2008

Purchasing Scheme

The new Acquisitions Scheme for member museums is established, the first purchases included work by Emily Wardill, Rosalind Nashashibi, Seamus Harahan and Lindsay Seers.

Gift

From 2008 onwards more than 300 modern and contemporary works are distributed to member museums by the Contemporary Art Society from The Eric & Jean Cass Gift. This included work by Karel Appel, Michael Craig-Martin, Barbara Hepworth, Joan Miro, Henry Moore, Victor Pasmore, Eduardo Paolozzi, Pablo Picasso and Niki de Saint-Phalle.

2009

Annual Award

Launch of the new Annual Award for Museums – Commission to Collect, providing £60,000 to a selected member museum each year to commission a new work by a contemporary artist for their collection. The selection panel in 2009 included Rosalind Nashashibi, Olivia Plender and Martin Boyce.

National Network

The National Network, the Subject Specialist Network for contemporary art is launched. It provides museum and arts professionals with a programme of seminars, workshops and international trips to enable knowledge sharing and the generation of new ideas with regards to public collection development.

2010

Centenary

The Contemporary Art Society celebrates its Centenary Year with a year-long programme of displays and events across the country. The publication *What's Next? 100 Years of the Contemporary Art Society* followed in 2012.

Phyllida Barlow, *Untitled: Disaster III*, 2010, sculpture: plywood, fabrics, wire netting, polystyrene, cardboard, scrim, cement, bonding plaster, sealant, dust, paint, spray paint, castors, 60 x 90 x 75 cm, Collection of Nottingham Castle Museum & Art Gallery © Phyllida Barlow. Courtesy the artist and Hauser & Wirth.

Chairman

Mark Stephens becomes Chairman (until 2014).

2011

Purchase

Three works by Phyllida Barlow are presented, with support from The Art Fund, to Nottingham Castle Museum & Art Gallery: *Untitled: Disaster III* (2010), *Untitled: Basel structure* (2010) and *Untitled: Crushed shape* (2011).

Gift

David Hockney, *A Rake's Progress* (1961–63), portfolio of sixteen prints, etching and acquatint, is bequeathed by Dr. Roland Lande to Whitworth Art Gallery in memory of his life partner Walter Urech.

2012

Premises

The Contemporary Art Society moves into new premises designed by Carmody Groarke at 59 Central Street, Clerkenwell, with a new programme of talks and displays showing work purchased and gifted to museums and showcasing the work of artist members.

Gift

Elizabeth Price, USER GROUP DISCO (2009), HD video, is presented to Scottish National Gallery of Modern Art, Edinburgh, through support of the Contemporary Art Society's Annual Fundraiser.

Annual Award

Oliver Laric wins the 2012 Annual Award with The Collection and Usher Gallery, Lincoln. Laric 3D scans objects from Lincoln's collection, making them available to download and use without copyright restrictions from lincoln3dscans.co.uk.

2013

Director

Caroline Douglas becomes Director.

Annual Award

Elizabeth Price wins the 2013 Annual Award with The Ashmolean Museum of Art and Archaeology, University of Oxford, in partnership with the Pitt Rivers Museum and the Ruskin School of Art. The work will be the first moving image work by a living artist to be acquired by The Ashmolean.

2014

Purchasing Scheme

Launch of the new craft scheme, The Omega Fund, named after the Omega Workshops established by Roger Fry and members of the Bloomsbury Group whose aim was to blur the boundaries between art and craft. The fund has a specific focus on emerging makers.

Contributor Biographies

Anna Colin is a curator and writer based in London. She is a co-founder and director of Open School East, a non-fee paying study programme, which launched in 2013 in east London. She is also associate curator at Fondation Galeries Lafayette in Paris and the co-curator, with Lydia Yee, of the 'British Art Show 8'. She has curated exhibitions and projects in spaces including Le Quartier, contemporary art centre of Quimper; La Synagogue de Delme; Galleria d'Arte Moderna, Turin; Contemporary Image Collective, Cairo; la Maison populaire, Montreuil; and The Women's Library, London. She was co-director of Bétonsalon, Paris in 2011–12, and curator at Gasworks, London, in 2007–10, where she worked on exhibitions with artists including Matthew Darbyshire, Olivia Plender, The Otolith Group and Martin Beck.

Matthew Darbyshire was born in the UK in 1977, and lives and works in Rochester, Kent. He studied Fine Art at the Slade School of Art and at the Royal Academy Schools in London. He is best known for installations that draw heavily on the aesthetic language of today's commodity culture and the aspirational lifestyles it promotes. His work explores design as a barometer of social change within the complex visual environment of contemporary Britain. Recent exhibitions include those at The Hepworth, Wakefield (2014), Bloomberg, London (2013), Tramway, Glasgow (2012), The Hayward Project Space, London (2009), Gasworks, London (2008). He has participated in numerous group exhibitions across Europe, Asia and America, and in major UK survey shows, including the 'British Art Show 7', 'Days of the Comet' (2010) and Tate Britain's Triennial 'Altermodern' (2009).

Helen Kaplinsky is an independent curator and writer based in London. She has worked with the Arts Council Collection since 2011, having been awarded an opportunity to curate the collection while studying on the Curating MFA at Goldsmiths University in 2009–11. Curatorial projects and exhibitions include a residency with Flux Factory in New York, and 'Image as Witness', 'Thrall'dom' at LIMAZULU, and 'Auto Couture', all in London. She lectures in Art and Design History at City Literary Institute, and has undertaken residencies at Treignac Projet in France, Sichuan Fine Art Institute and 501 Artspace, in China, and Islington Mill, London.

Helen Rees Leahy is Senior Lecturer and Director of the Centre of Museology at the University of Manchester, where she teaches on the MA in Art Gallery and Museum Studies. Previously, she worked as a curator and museum director for over 12 years, and has organised numerous exhibitions of fine art and design. She writes on topics relating to practices of individual and institutional collecting, in both historical and contemporary contexts, including issues of patronage, display and interpretation. She recently published *Museum Bodies* (Ashgate, 2012) and is currently working on a major new project, 'The Critical Lives of Exhibitions', which explores the archives, afterlives, and reputations of art exhibitions. She is also Curatorial Consultant to Elizabeth Gaskell's House, a new house museum in the restored nineteenth century Manchester home of the novelist and her family, which will open in October 2014.

Ingrid Swenson has been Director of PEER in London (formerly The Pier Trust) since 1998 and has curated over 50 gallery and public realm projects with a wide range of artists, including Martin Creed, Mike Nelson, Siobhan Hapaska, Breda Beban, Tania Kovats, Bob and Roberta Smith, Anthony McCall, John Frankland, Kathy Prendergast, John Smith, Stuart Brisley, Keith Coventry and Karin Ruggaber. Prior to PEER she worked in a wide range of museums, galleries and arts organisations including the ICA (as exhibitions coordinator 1988– 2004), and on specific projects for the Serpentine Gallery, the Whitechapel Gallery, the Contemporary Art Society, RSA and others.

Gaia Tedone is a curator based in London. She holds an MFA in Curating from Goldsmiths College, London, and was a curatorial fellow of the Whitney Independent Study Program, New York. She has worked at Tate Modern, assisting on acquisitions and displays for the Collection of Photography and International Art, and was an Assistant Curator for the David Roberts Art Foundation in London (2008–10). Past curatorial projects include: 'Shifting Gazes' (Guest Projects, London, 2013; with Christine Takengny), 'Is Seeing Believing?' (or-bits.com, TRUTH, 2011), 'Foreclosed. Between Crisis and Possibility' (The Kitchen, New York, 2011; with ISP fellows Jennifer Burris, Sofía Olascoaga, Sadia Shirazi), 'Nervous System' (James Taylor Gallery, London, 2009), 'Every Story is a Travel Story' (Candid Arts Trust, London, 2008).

Acknowledgements

The Contemporary Art Society and Whitechapel Gallery would like to thank Arts Council England for its generous support of this collaborative project.

Contemporary Art Society
The Contemporary Art Society would like to thank the following supporters for their vital and generous support of our work to develop public collections across the UK.

Collections Committee 2013–2014
Cathy Wills (Chair), Hugo Brown, Loraine da Costa, Donall Curtin, Chris Jermyn, Françoise Sarre Rapp, Paul Smith, Audrey Wallrock, and Michael Webber.

Collections Patrons 2013–2014
Diane Abela, Marie Elena Angulo & Henry Zarb, Heidi Baravalle, Elizabeth Bauza, Robert Bensoussan, Anette Bollag-Rothschild, Michael & Philippa Bradley, Hugo Brown, Simone Brych-Nourry, Bertrand Coste, Laurence Coste, Loraine da Costa, Donall Curtin, Sophie Diedrichs-Cox, Valentina Drouin, Sarah Elson, Antje & Andrew Géczy, David & Susan Gilbert, Kira Heuer, Helen Janecek, Chris Jermyn, Linda Keyte, Paula Lent, Yves & Martina Klemmer, Keith Morris & Catherine Mason, Suling Mead, Alexandra Nash, Flavia Nespatti, Simon & Midge Palley, Veronique Parke, Daniele Pescali, Mark Renton, Susan Rosenberg, Françoise Sarre Rapp, Dasha Shenkman, Brian Smith, Paul Smith, Glenn & Gaby Unterhalter, Audrey Wallrock, Michael Webber, Cathy Wills, Edwin & Dina Wulfsohn, Anna Yang & Joseph Schull, Andrzej & Jill Zarzycki.

Centenary Patrons 2013–2014
Nicola Blake, Alla & Bill Broeksmit, Jeffrey Boone, Paul & Gisele Caseiras, Wolf & Carol Cesman, Susie Cochin de Billy, Daniela Colaiacovo, Tommaso Corvi-Mora, Theo Danjuma, Jonathan & Jacqueline Gestetner, Karina el Helou, Marcelle Joseph, Michael & Fiona King, Audrey Klein, Anna Lapshina, Zach & Julia Leonard, Joanna Mackiewicz-Gemes, Amber Mahood, Paul McKeown, Frederique Pierre Pierre, Mariela Pissioti, Will Ramsay, Karsten Schubert, Dan & Ellen Shapiro, Henrietta Shields, Karen Smith, Dr. Richard Sykes & Penny Mason, Salavat Timiryasov and Susie Tinsley.

Honorary Patrons
Tiqui Atencio, Nicholas Berwin, Eric & Jean Cass, Frank Cohen, Denise Esfandi, James Hughes-Hallett, Costas Kaplanis, Fatima & Eskandar Maleki, Alison Myners, Valeria Napoleone, Simon Turner, Nicky Wilson, and Anita Zabludowicz.
And others who wish to remain anonymous.

We remain grateful for the ongoing support of the Contemporary Art Society by Arts Council England.

Contemporary Art Society Trustees:
Mark Stephens CBE, Javid Cante, Tommaso Corvi-Mora, Sarah Elson, Antje Géczy, David Gilbert, Zach Leonard, Keith Morris, Cathy Wills, and Edwin Wulfsohn.

Contemporary Art Society Staff:
Director: Caroline Douglas
Deputy Director: Sophia Bardsley

Phil Ashcroft, Victoria Avery, Lucy Bayley, Will Davis, Robert Dingle, Mark Doyle, Matthew Hearn, Frances Hetherington, Moira Innes, Jordan Kaplan, Miriam Metliss, Kate Moirali, Fabienne Nicholas, Grace O'Connor, Jenny Prytherch, Helen Nisbet, Sarah Page, Dida Tait, Christine Takengny, Kelly Tsipni-Kolaza, Ellen Mara De Wachter, Jeni Walwin, and Kay Watson.

Whitechapel Art Gallery

The Whitechapel Gallery thanks its supporters, whose generosity enables the Gallery to realise its pioneering programmes.
Whitechapel Gallery Director's Circle
The Ampersand Foundation, Ivor and Sarah Braka, Aud and Paolo Cuniberti, D. Daskalopoulos Collection (Greece), Joseph and Marie Donnelly, Maryam and Edward Eisler, Peter and Maria Kellner, Marian Goodman Gallery, Yana and Stephen Peel, Catherine and Franck Petitgas, SAHA (Istanbul), Muriel and Freddy Salem, Anita and Poju Zabludowicz and those who wish to remain anonymous.

Whitechapel Gallery Curator's Circle
Erin Bell and Michael Cohen, Nicholas Berwin Charitable Trust, Ida Levine, the Loveday Family, Adrian and Jennifer O'Carroll, Jonathan Tyler and those who wish to remain anonymous.

Whitechapel Gallery Patrons
Ursula and Ray van Almsick, Malgosia Alterman, Vanessa Arelle, Charlotte and Alan Artus, Hugo Brown, Sadie Coles HQ, Swantje Conrad, Alastair Cookson, Donall Curtin, Miel de Botton, Maria de Madariaga, Dunnett Craven Ltd, Jeff and Jennifer Eldredge, Louis and Sarah Elson, Alan and Joanna Gemes, Isabelle Hotimsky, Amrita Jhaveri, Sigrid Kirk, Anna Lapshina, Victor and Anne Lewis, Scott Mead, Jon and Amanda Moore, Bozena Nelhams, Maureen Paley, Dominic Palfreyman, The Porter Foundation, Jasmin Pelham, Mariela Pissioti, The Porter Foundation, Lauren Prakke, Alice Rawsthorn, Jon Ridgway, Alex Sainsbury and Elinor Jansz, Kaveh and Cora Sheibani, Bina and Philippe von Stauffenberg, Hugh and Catherine Stevenson, Tom Symes, Helen Thorpe (The Helen Randag Charitable Foundation), Christoph and Marion Trestler, Emily Tsingou and Henry Bond, Audrey Wallrock, Kevin Walters, Susan Whiteley, Roberta S Wolens and those who wish to remain anonymous.

The American Friends of the Whitechapel Gallery
Dick and Betsy DeVos Family Foundation, Ambassador and Mrs Louis B Susman and those who wish to remain anonymous.

Whitechapel Gallery First Futures
Jam Acuzar, Sharifa Alsudairi, Katharine Arnold, Maria Arones, John Auerbach, Edouard Benveniste-Schuler, Fiorina Benveniste-Schuler, Natalia Blaskovicova, Ingrid Chen, Bianca Chu, Nathaniel Clark, Tom Cole, Jonathan Crockett, Celia Davidson, Stéphanie de Preux Dominicé, Alessandro Diotallevi, Michelle D'Souza, Christopher Fields and Brendan Olley, Laura Ghazzaoui, Geraldine Guyot, Lawrence van Hagen, Asli Hatipoglu, Constantin Hemmerle, Carolyn Hodler, Katherine Holmgren, Zoe Karafylakis Sperling, Deborah Kattan, Tamila Kerimova, Benjamin Khalili, Rasha Khawaja, Frank Krikhaar, Aliki Lampropoulos, Alexandra Lefort, Arianne Levene Piper, Georgina Lewis, Alex Logsdail, Julia Magee, Kristina McLean, Paul Miliotis, Janna Miller, Gloria Monfrini, Indi Oliver, Yuki Oshima Wilpon, Katharina Ottmann, Juan Pepa, Josephine von Perfall, Alexander V Petalas, Hannah Philp, Patricia Pratas, Maria Cruz Rashidan, Eugenio Re Rebaudengo, Daniela Sanchez, Paola Saracino Fendi, Henrietta Shields, Marie-Anya Shriro, Max Silver, Yassi Sohrabi, Alexander Stamatiadis, Roxana Sursock Karam, Gerald Tan, Edward Tang, Julia Tarasyuk, Billal Taright, Nayrouz Tatanaki, Abdullah Al Turki, Giacomo Vigliar, Rosanna Widen, Andrea Wild Botero and those who wish to remain anonymous.

Whitechapel Gallery Associates
Ariane Braillard and Francesco Cincotta, Beverley Buckingham, Salima Chebbah, Christian Erlandson and Reagan Kiser, Lyn Fuss, David Killick, Laetitia Lina, John Newbigin, Noble Savage Property, Chandrakant Patel, Fozia Rizvi, Fabio Rossi and Elaine W Ng, David Ryder, Cherrill and Ian Scheer, Karsten Schubert and all those who wish to remain anonymous.

We remain grateful for the ongoing support of Whitechapel Gallery Members and Arts Council England.

Whitechapel Gallery Trustees
Chairman of the Trustees: Robert Taylor

Duncan Ackery, Swantje Conrad, Maryam Eisler, Ann Gallagher, Anupam Ganguli, Runa Islam, Michael Keith, Rania Khan, Cornelius Medvei, Farshid Moussavi, Dominic Palfreyman, Catherine Petitgas, Alice Rawsthorn, Andrea Rose, Rohan Silva, John Smith, Alasdhair Willis.

Whitechapel Gallery Staff
Director: Iwona Blazwick
Managing Director: Stephen Crampton-Hayward
Anne Akello-Otema, Verissa Akoto, Chris Aldgate, Sarah Auld, Sarah Barrett, Safwan Bazara, Katrina Black, Antonia Blocker, Poppy Bowers, Jussi Brightmore, Gino Brignoli, Emily Butler, Vicky Carmichael, Nathaniel Cary, Paul Crook, Emma Defoe, Dan Eaglesham, Elizabeth Evans, Sue Evans, Tom Fleming, Michele Fletcher, Alison Gannagé-Addison Atkinson, Tim Gosden, Gary Haines, Hannah Harewood, Bryony Harris, Clare Hawkins, Rebecca Head, Chiara Heal, Daniel Herrmann, Quay Hoang, Alice Hubley, Richard Johnson, Omar Kholeif, Lorna Killin, James Knight, Miles Lauterwasser, Alexandra Lawson, Patrick Lears, Selina Levinson, Daisy Mallabar, Rachel Mapplebeck, Sandie Mattioli, Lucy May, Jo Melvin, Deya Mukherjee, Maggie Nightingale, Thomas Ogden, Alex O'Neill, Dominic Peach, Magnus af Petersens, Patricia Pisanelli, Darryl de Prez, Habda Rashid, Pamela Sepulveda, Harpreet Sharma, Kathryn Simpson, Marijke Steedman, Candy Stobbs, Sophie Thornberry, Aharon Tomlin, Imogen Topliss, Sofia Victorino, Thom Walker, Jonathan Weston, Nayia Yiakoumaki, Andrea Ziemer.

The Contemporary Art Society and the Whitechapel Gallery would like to warmly thank Curatorial Fellows Anna Colin, Helen Kaplinsky, Ingrid Swenson and Gaia Tedone; all the lenders and their staff, the host museums and the touring venues. We would also like to thank Lucy Byatt, Paul Hobson and Kirsty Ogg for their vision in initiating this collaborative project. We would also like to thank Justine Schuster and Stuart Smith for designing and producing this publication.

Anna Colin
I would like to extend my sincere thanks to: Richard Burns, Bury Art Gallery and Museum; Emma Heslewood, Lindsey McCormick and Alexandra Walker, Harris Museum & Art Gallery; Tom Ireland, Grundy Art Gallery; Moira Lindsay, Victoria Gallery & Museum; David Morris and Helen Stalker, Whitworth Art Gallery; Nick Rogers, James Arnold and Beth Hughes, Abbot Hall Art Gallery; Grant Scanlan, Huddersfield Art Gallery; Colin Simpson, Williamson Art Gallery and Museum; Richard Smith, Peter Scott Gallery; Nigel Walsh, Leeds Art Gallery; Matthew Watson, Bolton Museum; Hannah Williamson and Ruth Shrigley, Manchester Art Gallery; Lucy Bayley and Robert Dingle, Contemporary Art Society; Kirsty Ogg, Candy Stobbs and Paula Morison, Whitechapel Gallery; and Maurice Carlin, Alex Farquharson, Jerry Parke and Tom Steele.

Helen Kaplinsky
Staff at Museums and Galleries on the East Coast including: Norwich Castle, Lincoln Collection and Usher Gallery, Hatton Gallery, The Laing, Shipley, Tennyson Research Centre in Lincoln, The Live Art Archives – University of Bristol and Hull College of Art and Design from whom we borrowed the Hull Time Based Art material, my host museum Ferens Art Gallery in Hull and tour partner mima. As well as artists Heath Bunting, Simon Poulter, Fran Cottell and Jan Howarth whose work is not represented in the collections but I borrowed from directly. In addition thanks for development of the exhibition, public programme and catalogue essay to Ian Waites, Kirsty Ogg, Marjorie Allthorpe-Guyton, Sarah Moulden, Mike Stubbs, Katrina Sluis, Beryl Graham, Ele Carpenter and Marysia Lewandowska – who first piqued my interest in 'the commons'.

Gaia Tedone
I wish to express my sincere gratitude to: Jenny Lund, Suzie Plumb, Alexia Lazou and Kevin Bacon, Brighton & Hove Museums; Sanna Moore and Sara Cooper, Towner; Frank Gray and Jane King, Screen Archive South East; George Auckland, Lester Smith, Stephen Herbert and Bill Barnes, The Magic Lantern Society; Donata Pesenti, Roberta Basano and Raffaella Isoardi, Museo Nazionale del Cinema in Turin; Sarah Wilde, BFI; Tim Craven, Southampton City Art Gallery; Toni Booth, National Media Museum Bradford; Charlotte Samuels, Kingston Museum; Matthew Lee, Imperial War Museum; Sophie Cummings, Swindon Museum; Julian Warren, Bristol Record Office; Catherine Littlejohns and Julia Carver, Bristol Museums. My special thanks to all the artists and performers involved in the exhibition and public programme.

Ingrid Swenson
I would like to express my thanks and gratitude to the many individuals I met during my research in the Midlands, who all gave very generously of their time and knowledge. In particular Marguerite Nugent and Corinne Miller, Wolverhampton Art Gallery; Sarah Shalgosky, the University of Warwick Art Collection; Jane May, New Walk Museum and Art Gallery, Leicester; Pamela Wood, Nottingham Museum and Art Gallery, Miranda Goodby and Jean Milton, The Potteries Museum and Art Gallery, Stoke-on-Trent; Stephen Snoddy, The New Art Gallery, Walsall; Martin Roberts and Chris Kirby, The Herbert Art Gallery and Museum, Coventry; Ben Miller, Wedgwood Museum and Alice Swatton, Leamington Spa Art Gallery and Museum. Paul Scott for his loans to the display, contributing ideas in the essay, and for taking part in the symposium along with Tanya Harrod, Matthew Darbyshire, Sarah Shalgosky and finally, Jess Litherland with whom I have enjoyed our wider discussions about the project and tour to Rugby Art Gallery and Museum.

Published in 2014 by the Contemporary Art Society and Whitechapel Gallery on the occasion of the following series of displays:

Nothing Beautiful Unless Useful
17 September – 1 December 2013

Damn braces: Bless relaxes
10 December 2013 – 9 March 2014

The Best is Not Too Good for You
18 March – 1 June 2014

Twixt Two Worlds
11 June – 31 August 2014

Contemporary Art Society
59 Central Street
London EC1V 3AF
United Kingdom
contemporaryartsociety.org

Whitechapel Gallery
77–82 Whitechapel High Street
London E1 7QX
United Kingdom
whitechapelgallery.org

Displays organised by the Whitechapel Gallery, London
Curators: Kirsty Ogg and Omar Kholeif
Assistant Curator: Candy Stobbs with assistance from
Natalie Craven, Paula Morison and Jonathan Weston
Installation: Patrick Lears and Nathaniel Cary
AV Coordination: Richard Johnson
Public Programme: Antonia Blocker and Sofia Victorino

Fellowship and Touring Displays organised by the Contemporary Art Society
Displays Programme Manager: Lucy Bayley
Museum Acquisition and Public Programmes Manager: Christine Takengny
Displays Programme (maternity cover): Karen Di Franco
Public Programme: Robert Dingle
Communications: Jenny Prytherch

Publication
Edited by the Contemporary Art Society and Whitechapel Gallery
Copy-editing: Gerrie Van Noord
Image and chronology research: Kay Watson
Design by SMITH
Alice Austin, Allon Kaye, Justine Schuster
Printed by Castelli Bolis Poligrafiche
© the authors, artists, photographers, Whitechapel Gallery Ventures Limited

ISBN: 978-0-85488-229-8
To order (UK and Europe)
call +44 (0)202 7522 7888 or
mailorder@whitechapelgallery.org

Distributed to the book trade
(UK & Europe) by Central Books
www.centralbooks.com

Represented in Europe by Durnell Marketing
orders@durnell.co.uk

This publication is made possible by Arts Council England.

Supported using public funding by
ARTS COUNCIL ENGLAND

The Paul Mellon Centre *for Studies in British Art*

contemporary art society

Whitechapel Gallery

Host and Tour Partners

Harris Museum & Art Gallery

Hull City Council

UNIVERSITY OF LIVERPOOL

mima middlesbrough institute of modern art

Royal Pavilion & Museums

RUGBY ART GALLERY & MUSEUM

towner

VG&M
VICTORIA GALLERY & MUSEUM

WAVE
THE MUSEUMS, GALLERIES & ARCHIVES OF WOLVERHAMPTON